TREASURED VOLUME OF PRAYERS

By the same author

TREASURED VOLUME OF POEMS

TREASURED VOLUME OF THOUGHTS

Treasured Volume of

PRAYERS

an anthology collected by

John Scott

An Oak Tree Press Book
PUBLISHED BY
THE C. R. GIBSON COMPANY
NORWALK, CONNECTICUT

© Copyright, MCMLXX, by John Scott
Library of Congress Catalog Card Number: 76-104722
Printed in the United States of America
All Rights Reserved

dedicated to the loving memory of my father

Big Jack

. . . but first, a word

HERE should be nothing strange in a collection of prayers by a broadcaster. From the earliest days of radio there have been prayers and sermons on the air, and choirs great and humble have sung the praise of God through the microphone. Most recently the whole world listened as a Psalm went up to God from the Moon— when man at his highest once more recognized the All-Highest.

I do not know when I first became aware of the analogy between prayer and broadcasting. It's a poor analogy, but there it is: the word spoken, speeding instantly, invisibly, to a distant ear. One cannot, of course compare the ordinary business of radio with the sacred affair of prayer. The broadcaster reaches for many distant ears; he who prays seeks One Who is never distant.

The object of this book is to bring together in one volume a collection of prayers, most of which will be useful to most readers. All are in the Judaeo-Christian tradition—the tradition of the Holy Bible. They include selections from many churches in that tradition which recognizes the Fatherhood of One God. They show, surprisingly, how

[7]

much all His sons and daughters speak the same language when they pray to Him—praising Him, or seeking His help.

These are prayers for all occasions, not excepting the occasion of daily prayer. But here, too, are some of the great prayers of our common history. One or two selections may have little more than historical interest, but they show how the history of prayer has continued from the Psalmist to the Space Age.

It is not possible to say the proper words of thanks for the eminent churchmen of our day whose prayers have been selected for this *Treasured Volume*. But they did not give me the privilege of including them as a gesture to me: they are for you, and the greater glory of God.

Some of the prayers are covered by existing copyright and credit for permission to use them is given, gratefully, to The Central Conference of American Rabbis, publishers of *The Union Home Prayer Book*, and to the Bloch Publishing Company, publishers of the compendious *Authorized Daily Prayer Book*, by Joseph H. Hertz.

For the Psalms which are included, I have used the text of the King James version.

Some prayers, including selections from *The Book of Common Prayer*—will be familiar. No collection of prayers would be complete without those which have been said so frequently that their words— in the line of the poet Ya'aqov Cohen—well "know the heavenly paths."

The order I have followed is simple, following the calendar—from New Year's Day, through the Spring, the Summer days of weddings and vacations, and the Fall, to Christmas and the year's end. Interspersed, by design, are general or daily prayers, since such prayers are always in season, as long as "God's in His heaven" and "all's right with the world."

JOHN SCOTT

TREASURED VOLUME OF PRAYERS

THE LORD'S PRAYER

The Lord's Prayer, or "Our Father" as it is known from its first two words ("Pater Noster" in Latin) is probably the most universally used prayer in the world. It is derived from the words of Jesus in the New Testament. There are variations in the words of this prayer. This is understandable since the two versions in the New Testament—of Matthew and Luke—do not themselves agree. For example, the word "debtors" as contrasted with "those who trespass against us" is from Matthew—and "debtors" is probably the best translation. However, in the following version, I have used the phrases best known to most Christians, confident that those who are familiar with one version or another will—from the habit of prayer—use their own accustomed words. As for the doxology at the conclusion ("For thine is . . ." etc.) the experts agree that this was a common Jewish praise of God which the early Christians continued to use at the end of the prayer. It continued in use in the early Christian churches in the East. Presumably devout men who spent their lives writing out the Scriptures in long-hand, and knowing the prayer by heart, unconsciously inserted it into some of the early copies of Scripture. That is how, presumably again, it found its way into the "King James' version" of the Bible and into a common version of the prayer. The latest translations of the New Testament do not include the traditional lines in the text, but the words are included here because of their long use—going back almost two thousand years—and the simple fact that no one can possibly object to any praise of God at any time.

OUR FATHER, Who art in heaven, hallowed be Thy Name. Thy kingdom come. Thy will be done on earth, as it is in heaven. Give us this day our daily bread. And forgive us our trespasses, as we forgive those who trespass against us. And lead us not into temptation, but deliver us from evil.

For Thine is the kingdom and the power and the glory for ever and ever. Amen.

PRAYER FOR A NEW YEAR

BLESS this year unto us, O Lord our God, together with every kind of the produce thereof, for our welfare; give dew and rain for a blessing upon the face of the earth. O satisfy us with Thy goodness, and bless our year like other good years. Blessed art Thou, O Lord, who blessest the years. Amen.

NEW YEAR'S PRAYER

O THOU, Who are ever the same, grant us to pass through the coming year with faithful hearts, that we may be able in all things to please Thy loving eyes. Amen.

PRAYER FOR JANUARY FIRST

ALMIGHTY GOD, Who madest Thy blessed Son to be circumcised, and obedient to the law for man; grant us the true circumcision of the spirit; that, our hearts, and all our members, being mortified from all worldly and carnal lusts, we may in all things obey Thy blessed will; through the same Thy Son Jesus Christ our Lord. Amen.

MORNING PRAYER

ALMIGHTY and most merciful Father; we have erred, and strayed from Thy ways like lost sheep. We have followed too much the devices and desires of our own hearts. We have offended against Thy holy laws. We have left undone those things which we ought to have done; and we have done those things which we ought not to have done; and there is no health in us. But Thou, O Lord, have mercy upon us, miserable offenders. Spare Thou those, O God, who confess their faults. Restore Thou those who are penitent; according to Thy promises declared unto mankind in Christ Jesus our Lord. And grant, O most merciful Father, for His sake; that we may hereafter live a godly, righteous, and sober life, to the glory of Thy holy Name. Amen.

NIGHT PRAYER

MY GOD! I thank Thee for having brought me safely through this day, and I implore Thee to watch over me also during this night, and to preserve me from every sin. I dedicate to Thee all my sleep, that with every breath I draw, I may praise Thee, thank Thee, and love Thee as the saints do in paradise.

GRACE BEFORE MEALS

BLESS TO US, O Lord, these Thy good creatures, which we are now about to receive. Give them strength to nourish us, and us grace to serve Thee, through Jesus Christ our Lord. Amen.

GRACE AFTER MEALS

WE ACKNOWLEDGE, O God, our dependence upon Thee, and we give Thee thanks for feeding us at this time, and for all other benefits, through Jesus Christ our Lord. Amen.

PSALM 70

MAKE HASTE, O God, to deliver me; make haste to help me, O Lord.

Let them be ashamed and confounded that seek after my soul: let them be turned backward, and put to confusion, that desire my hurt.

Let them be turned back for a reward of their shame that say, Aha, aha.

Let all those that seek Thee rejoice and be glad in Thee: and let such as love Thy salvation say continually, Let God be magnified.

But I am poor and needy; make haste unto me, O God: Thou art my help and my deliverer; O Lord, make no tarrying.

PRAYER FOR A
MORE PERFECT LIFE

Thomas a Kempis, *author of this prayer, was a German-born Dutch monk. He is internationally famous for the* Imitation of Christ, *a book of meditations and prayers which is still widely used today—500 years after it was first published.*

O Lord, Thou knowest what is best for us, let this or that be done, as Thou shalt please. Give what Thou wilt, and how much Thou wilt, and when Thou wilt. Deal with me as Thou thinkest good, and as best pleaseth Thee. Set me where Thou wilt, and deal with me in all things just as Thou wilt. Behold, I am Thy servant, prepared for all things; for I desire not to live unto myself, but unto Thee; and Oh, that I could do it worthily and perfectly! Amen.

PRAYER FOR SUSTENANCE

My help is from the Lord, Who made heaven and earth. Cast thy burden upon the Lord, and He shall sustain thee. Mark the innocent man, and behold the upright; for the latter end of that man is peace. Trust in the Lord, and do good; dwell in the land, and feed upon faithfulness. Behold, God is my salvation; I will trust and will not be afraid: for the Lord God is my strength and song, and He is become my salvation. O Sovereign of the universe, in Thy holy words it is written, saying, He that trusteth in the Lord, loving-kindness shall compass him about; and it is written, And Thou givest life to them all. O Lord God of truth, send blessing and prosperity upon all the work of my hands, for I trust in Thee that Thou wilt so bless me through my occupation and calling, that I may be enabled to support myself and the members of my household with ease and not with pain, by lawful and not by forbidden means, unto life and peace. In me also let the scripture be fulfilled, Cast thy burden upon the Lord, and He shall sustain thee. Amen.

PRAYER FOR THE SABBATH

RAISED BE Thy name for ever, O our King, the great and holy God and King, in heaven and on earth; for unto Thee, O Lord our God, and God of our fathers, song and praise are becoming, hymn and psalm, strength and dominion, victory, greatness and might, renown and glory, holiness and sovereignty, blessings and thanksgivings from henceforth even for ever. Blessed art Thou, O Lord, God and King, great in praises, God of thanksgivings, Lord of wonders, Who makest choice of song and psalm, O King and God, the Life of all worlds.

Blessed is the Lord, Who is to be blessed for ever and ever.

Blessed art Thou, O Lord our God, King of the Universe, Who formest light and createst darkness, Who makest peace and createst all things: Who in mercy givest light to the earth and to them that dwell thereon, and in Thy goodness renewest the creation every day continually. How manifold are Thy works, O Lord! In wisdom hast Thou made them all: the earth is full of Thy possessions. O King, Who alone wast exalted from aforetime, praised, glorified and extolled from days of old; O everlasting God, in Thine abundant mercies, have mercy upon us, Lord of our strength, Rock of our stronghold, Shield of our salvation, Thou Stronghold of ours!

The blessed God, great in knowledge, prepared and formed the rays of the sun: it was a boon He produced as a glory to His Name: He set the luminaries around about His strength. The chiefs of His hosts are holy beings that exalt the Almighty, and continually declare the glory of God and His holiness. Be Thou blessed, O Lord our God, for the excellency of Thy handiwork, and for the bright luminaries which Thou hast made: they shall glorify Thee for ever.

PRAYER FOR CLOSER COMMUNION WITH GOD

This prayer by the REVEREND DOCTOR BILLY GRAHAM *echoes the Bible he preaches in his crusades across the Western World, and mirrors the fundamentals of the faith which sustains him.*

UR FATHER GOD, we come to Thee
With closed eyes but open hearts;
Well realizing that what You desire for us
Is far better than what we want for ourselves.
For, "As the heavens are far above the earth,
So are Your ways higher (and better) than our ways."
Help us to realize that it is far better
To be deep and narrow,

Than to be broad and shallow.
And yet, give us tolerance and love
Toward those who have never been given
To see the Unseen and to know the Unknown.
Grant that our living make keep pace with our words,
That our tongues shall not move faster
Than our hearts.
Grant us the wisdom to build for eternity
Instead of time;
And to live every day as though You walked by our sides,
For You do.
In the Savior's Name we pray,
Amen.

A READER'S PRAYER

There is the story that the English essayist, Charles Lamb, once said he felt more like saying "Grace" before opening a good book than he did before meals. Lamb's jest inspired a thoughtful man, H. H. BARSTOW, to write the following prayer which was widely published in the past century.

ORD, let me never slight the meaning nor the moral of anything I read. Make me respect my mind so much that I dare not read what has no meaning nor moral. Help me choose with equal care my friends and my books, because they are both for life. Show me that as in a river, so in reading, the depths hold more of strength and beauty than the shallows. Teach me to value art without being blind to thought. Keep me from caring more for much reading than for careful reading; for books than the Book. Give me an ideal that will let me read only the best, and when that is done, stop me. Repay me with power to teach others, and then help me to say from a disciplined mind a grateful Amen.

PRAYER FOR HELP IN PRAYING

This prayer is by Francois Fénelon, *Archbishop of Cambray in France early in the 18th century—a man who won fame with his writings, royal displeasure for his liberal thought, and admiration by the serenity with which he took both the bitter and the sweet.*

Lord, I know not what I ought to ask of Thee; Thou only knowest what I need; Thou lovest me better than I know how to love myself. O Father! give to Thy child that which he himself knows not how to ask. I dare not ask either for crosses or consolations; I simply present myself before Thee, I open my heart to Thee. Behold my needs which I know not myself; see and do according to Thy tender mercy. Smite, or heal; depress me or raise me up; I adore all Thy purposes without knowing them; I am silent; I offer myself in sacrifice; I yield myself to Thee; I would have no other desire than to accomplish Thy will. Teach me to pray. Pray, Thyself, in me. Amen.

ET US PRAY—O most gracious God, our holy Father, of Whom the whole family in heaven and earth is named, Who givest all good gifts unto Thy children; we beseech Thee in behalf of this house, that Thou wouldst vouchsafe to bless, sanctify and hallow it with Thy continual presence. May health and sanctity, purity and humility, gentleness and obedience, the keeping of Thy laws and thanksgiving to God ever abide within these walls. Bless those who shall at any time occupy this house. Bless them in their going out and their coming in, in their duties and studies and recreations; in their food and rest; in their conversation and their silence; in their rising up and lying down; and grant that the words of their mouths and the meditations of their hearts may be always acceptable in Thy sight. Comfort them, O Lord, in sickness; sustain them in the inevitable sorrows of this transitory life, be with them in the hour of death and in the day of judgment. May angels of light here abide, henceforth to guard this dwelling and its inhabitants from all evil, through our Elder Brother, Thy Son, our Lord and Savior Jesus Christ. Amen.

PRAYER AGAINST
HARDNESS OF HEART

GRACIOUS FATHER, keep me through Thy Holy Spirit; keep my heart soft and tender now in health and amidst the bustle of the world; keep the thought of Thyself present to me as my Father in Jesus Christ; and keep alive in me a spirit of love and meekness to all men, that I may be at once gentle and active and firm. O strengthen me to bear pain, or sickness, or danger, or whatever Thou shalt be pleased to lay upon me, as Christ's soldier and servant; and let my faith overcome the world daily. Perfect and bless the work of Thy Spirit in the hearts of all Thy people, and may Thy kingdom come, and Thy will be done in earth as it is in heaven. I pray for this, and for all that Thou see to need, for Jesus Christ's sake. Amen.

PRAYER FOR
PEACE OF HEART

Lord God Almighty, Who art our true peace, and love eternal; enlighten our souls with the brightness of Thy peace, and purify our consciences with the sweetness of Thy love, that we may with peaceful hearts wait for the Author of Peace, and in the adversities of this world may ever have Thee for our guardian and protector; and so being fenced about by Thy care, may heartily give ourselves to the love of Thy peace. Amen.

PRAYER FOR
GOODNESS OF HEART

O God, the Father of our Savior, Jesus Christ, Whose Name is great, Whose nature is blissful, Whose goodness is inexhaustible, God and Ruler of all things Who art blessed forever; before Whom stand thousands and thousands, and ten thousand times ten thousand—the hosts of holy angels and arch-angels; sanctify O Lord, our souls and bodies and spirits, search our consciences, and cast out of us every evil thought, every base desire, all envy and pride, all wrath and anger, and all that is contrary to Thy holy will. And grant us, O Lord, Lover of men, with a pure heart and contrite soul, to call upon Thee, our holy God and Father Who are in heaven. Amen.

A BISHOP'S PRAYER

This is a prayer of His Excellency, Francis J. Mugavero, *Bishop of Brooklyn, the largest Roman Catholic Diocese in the nation. It is an eloquent reminder that all good ministers of God are themselves prayerful men regardless of title or rank. And it is readily adaptable to anyone by a simple substitution of vocation: for "bishop" use "carpenter," or "housewife," or "executive," or "chaplain."*

EAR God, Lord of this immense universe, its maker and supporter, penetrating, enveloping, yet infinitely transcend-ing it, Master of the vastness of space and of the intricate perfec-tion of the atom, and yet my Father, our Father, loving, kind, gentle and just, I come to you as a human being, a Christian, a bishop, a priest.

Help me to be a genuine human being, a true Christian, a good bishop and a faithful priest.

I beg Your blessing for all those toward whom I have any responsibility including, of course, my family, friends, acquaintances and associates. I want to pray for those of my own faith, those of other faiths, and those of no faith at all.

Bless my country, and grant that it may be upright, just and enlightened in its leaders, its policies and in its institutions.

I ask You in a special way to bring Your secret comfort and help to the unfortunate, the poor, the homeless, the lonely, the sick, the sorrowful, the persecuted, the dying, the oppressed. Stir up others and myself to be sincerely concerned about them and do whatever is humanly possible to help them.

Bless all men everywhere. Help us to love one another and to recognize in thought, word and deed that we are truly brothers. Help us to know and to love You Who are the loving Father of all.

MOTHER'S PRAYER
FOR A SICK BABY

This prayer in verse, from Elizabeth Barrett Browning's *"Isobel's Child," is a classic example of how close poetry is to prayer. Infused throughout with religious thought, it speaks eloquently for the mother who desires God's help.*

Dear Lord, Dear Lord!
Thou Who didst not erst deny
The mother-joy to Mary mild,
Blessèd in the blessèd Child,
Which hearkened in meek babyhood

[23]

Her cradle-hymn, albeit used
To that music interfused
In breasts of angels high and good!
Oh, take not, Lord, my babe away—
Oh, take not to Thy songful heaven,
The pretty baby Thou hast given.

PRAYER FOR
A SICK CHILD

O HEAVENLY FATHER, watch with us, we pray Thee, over the sick child for whom our prayers are offered, and grant that he/she may be restored to that perfect health which it is Thine alone to give; through Jesus Christ our Lord. Amen.

THANKSGIVING FOR
A CHILD'S RECOVERY
FROM ILLNESS

ALMIGHTY GOD and heavenly Father, we give Thee humble thanks for Thou hast been graciously pleased to deliver from his/her bodily sickness the child in whose behalf we bless and praise Thy Name, in the presence of all Thy people. Grant, we beseech Thee, O gracious Father, that he/she, through Thy help, may both faithfully live in this world according to Thy will, and also may be partaker of everlasting glory in the life to come; through Jesus Christ our Lord. Amen.

PRAYER FOR
BETTER UNDERSTANDING
OF SCRIPTURE

LESSED LORD, Who hast caused all holy Scriptures to be written for our learning; grant that we may in such wise hear them, read, mark, learn, and inwardly digest them, that by patience and comfort of Thy holy word, we may embrace, and ever hold fast, the blessed hope of everlasting life, which Thou hast given us in our Savior Jesus Christ. Amen.

THANKSGIVING FOR THE BIBLE

REVEREND DOCTOR ROBERT G. LEE, *pastor emeritus of the Bellevue Baptist Church, in Memphis, Tennessee, is the author of this prayer. Doctor Lee is a former president of the Southern Baptist Convention.*

GOD, our heavenly Father, we are grateful that we know from Thy blessed Book the truth that Thou art the high and lofty God Who inhabiteth eternity and yet art pleased to dwell with those who art of humble and contrite hearts.

We thank Thee for so many manifestations of Thy marvellous mercies. We thank Thee for Thy wonderful love manifested to us in so many ways and proved to us in that while we were yet sinners, Christ died for us—bearing our sins in His body on the cross of Calvary.

We thank Thee for the Bible—Thine infallible, inerrant, authoritative word—immeasurable in its influence, immortal in its hopes, inexhaustive in its adequacy, regenerative in power, personal in application, inspired in totality—the miracle Book of diversity in unity, of harmony in infinite complexity.

We thank Thee for the truth that Thy grace which bringeth salvation has appeared unto all men—teaching us that, denying ungodliness and worldly lusts, we should live soberly, righteously, and godly in this world, looking for that blessed hope and the glorious appearing of the great God and our Savior, Jesus Christ, Who gave Himself for us that He might redeem us from all iniquity, and purify unto Himself a peculiar people, zealous of good works.

Claiming no merit of our own, thanking Thee for cleansing us from all sins through Christ's blood, we ask Thee to help us to be well-pleasing unto Thee in all words and all deeds.

In Jesus' Name, Amen.

PRAYER FOR
JOY IN LIVING

H God! behold my grief and care. Fain would I serve Thee with a glad and cheerful countenance, but I cannot do it. However much I fight and struggle against my sadness, I am too weak for this sore conflict. Help me in my weakness, O Thou mighty God! and give me Thy Holy Spirit to refresh and comfort me in my sorrow. Amid all my fears and griefs I yet know that I am Thine in life and death, and that nothing can really part me from Thee; neither things present, nor things to come, neither trial, nor fear, nor pain. And therefore, O Lord, I will still trust in Thy grace. Thou wilt not send me away unheard. Sooner or later Thou wilt lift this burden from my heart and put a new song on my lips; and I will sing of Thy goodness, and thank and serve Thee here and for evermore. Amen.

A PRAYER FOR RECONCILING LOVE

The REVEREND DOCTOR RALPH W. SOCKMAN, *now minister emeritus at Christ Church (United Methodist) in New York, has had a long and varied career outside his pulpit—as an educator, author of several books, writer of a newspaper column, active member in many church organizations. This is his contribution.*

LMIGHTY and Eternal Father, in Whose law is our life and in Whose love is our hope, draw us so near to Thee in our thoughts that we may not be far from one another in our hearts. May the memory of Thy past mercies give us confidence in Thy future care. Make us ever mindful of the breadth and length and depth and height of that love which passeth knowledge and which from the cross prayed forgiveness for those who inflicted the pain. Help us to feel that we should love because Thou first loved us.

As we are exploring the earth, the sea and the heavens, reveal to us what we are missing through our dullness of eye, our littleness of spirit, our narrowness of mind, that we may find the fullness of life which Thy Son came to give. Make us wise enough to be simple, brave enough to be gentle, great enough to be modest and good enough to be generous in judgment and service. Give us the strength and will to bear our own burdens manfully and grant us the grace to bear one another's burdens and so fulfill the law of Christ.

O Lord, restrain the angry passions of men and reawaken the spirit of compassion that we may sympathise with those who suffer and see others as we wish them to see us. Shelter with Thy tender care the little ones of the world and guide with Thy strong counsel the leaders of the nations that Thy whole family may be freed from the insanity of war.

O God, help us to persevere as never before in the pursuit of peace until we find the paths to brotherhood. Amen.

PRAYER FOR AN
INCREASE IN CHARITY

GOD, Who hast taught us to do unto others as we would they should do unto us; give me grace to cleanse my heart and hands from all fraud and wrong, that I may hurt nobody by word or deed, but be true and just in all my dealings; that so, keeping innocency and taking heed unto the thing that is right, I may have peace at last; through Jesus Christ our Lord. Amen.

NCLINE, O LORD, Thy merciful ears, and illuminate the darkness of our hearts by the light of Thy visitation. Amen.

MAGNIFICAT

Y SOUL doth magnify the Lord, and my spirit hath rejoiced in God my Savior.

For He hath regarded the lowliness of His handmaiden.

For behold, from henceforth all generations shall call me blessed.

For He that is mighty hath magnified me; and holy is His Name.

And His mercy is on them that fear Him throughout all generations.

He hath showed strength with His arm; He hath scateered the proud in the imagination of their hearts.

He hath put down the mighty from their seat, and hath exalted the humble and meek.

He hath filled the hungry with good things; and the rich He hath sent empty away.

He, remembering His mercy, hath holpen His servant Israel; as He promised to our forefathers, Abraham and his seed for ever.

PRAYER IN
TIME OF TROUBLE

LL-WISE ruler of the destinies of man, out of the depths of my sorrow I cry unto Thee. Thou hast laid upon me a heavy burden and tried me with sorrow. Days of anguish and nights of weeping hast Thou meted out to me. Humbly I bow beneath Thy decree and try to accept Thy will. For what am I, but dust and ashes, that I should murmur against the wisdom of Thy ways? I feel that Thy decrees, though hard to bear, are meant for good and not for evil.

In the gloom around me, I look to Thee for light. Let me not seek in vain for Thy sustaining arm. Let me not rebel at Thy chastening, O Lord. Redeem me from faults and grant me strength to do Thy will with a perfect heart. Amen.

PRAYER FOR AN INCREASE
IN THE KNOWLEDGE OF GOD

St. Anselm, *Archbishop of Canterbury at the end of the 11th century, is the author of this prayer. He won his greatest fame as one of the earliest churchmen to apply reason to faith but he was also celebrated for his prayers—demonstrations of faith.*

God, Thou Who are life, wisdom, truth, bounty and blessedness, the eternal, the only true good! My God and my Lord, Thou art my hope and my heart's joy. I confess, with thanksgiving, that Thou has made me in Thine image, that I may direct all my thoughts to Thee, and love Thee. Lord, make me to know Thee aright, that I may more and more love, and enjoy, and possess Thee. And since, in the life here below, I cannot fully attain this blessedness, let it at least grow in me day by day, until it all be fulfilled at last in the life to come. Here be the knowledge of Thee increased, and there let it be perfected. Here let my love for Thee grow, and there let it ripen; that my joy being here great in hope, may there in fruition be made perfect.

STUDENTS' PRAYER

SAMUEL JOHNSON, *who wrote this prayer, is better known for writing an English dictionary and critical essays, but he wrote a whole volume of prayers and meditations. That he wrote from a heart which understood the trials of the classroom may be deduced from his own erratic schooling and the fact that he withdrew from Oxford before he earned his degree.*

LMIGHTY GOD, our heavenly Father, without Whose help labor is useless, without Whose light search is vain, invigorate my studies, and direct my inquiries, that I may, by due diligence and discernment, establish myself and others in Thy holy faith. Take not, O Lord, Thy holy spirit from me; let not evil thoughts have dominion in my mind. Let me not linger in ignorance, but enlighten and support me, for the sake of Jesus Christ, our Lord. Amen.

MORNING PRAYER

This comes from a 16th century primer

MERCIFUL Lord God, heavenly Father, I render most high laud, praise, and thanks unto Thee, that Thou has preserved me both this night, and all the times and days of my life hitherto, under Thy protection; and hast suffered me to live until this present hour. And I beseech Thee heartily that Thou wilt vouchsafe to receive me this day, and the residue of my whole life, from henceforth into Thy good keeping; ruling and governing me with Thy Holy Spirit, that all manner of darkness and evil may be utterly chased and driven out of my heart; and that I may walk in the light of Thy truth, to Thy glory and praise, and to the help and furtherance of my neighbor, through Jesus Christ our Lord and Savior. Amen.

NIGHT PRAYER

LIGHTEN our darkness, we beseech Thee, O Lord, and by Thy great mercy defend us from all perils and dangers of this night; for the love of Thy only Son, our Savior, Jesus Christ. Amen.

PRAYER IN TIME OF STORM

ALMIGHTY GOD, Lord of the storm and of the calm, the vexed sea and the quiet haven, of day and of night, of life and of death—grant unto us so to have our hearts stayed upon Thy faithfulness, Thine unchangingness and love, that whatsoever betide us, however black the cloud or dark the night, with quiet faith trusting in Thee, we may look upon Thee with untroubled eye, and walking in lowliness towards Thee, and in lovingness towards one another, abide all storms and troubles of this mortal life, beseeching that this may turn to the soul's true good. We ask it for Thy mercy's sake, shown in Jesus Christ our Lord. Amen.

[32]

DE PROFUNDIS

This is Psalm 130

UT OF the depths have I cried unto Thee, O Lord.
Lord, hear my voice: let Thine ears be attentive to the voice
of my supplications.

If Thou, Lord, shouldest mark iniquities, O Lord, who shall
stand?

But there is forgiveness with Thee, that Thou mayest be feared.

I wait for the Lord, my soul doth wait, and in His word do I
hope.

My soul waiteth for the Lord more than they that watch for
the morning: I say, more than they that watch for the morning.

Let Israel hope in the Lord, for with the Lord there is mercy,
and with Him is plenteous redemption.

And He shall redeem Israel from all his iniquities.

A PRAYER FOR THE SPACE AGE

This prayer was submitted by the REVEREND DOCTOR ROBERT I.
GANNON, S.J., *educator—former President of Fordham University, lecturer, author and currently Retreat Director at the Saint
Ignatius Retreat House operated by the Society of Jesus on Long
Island.*

S THE heavens open to us more and more, grant, dear
Lord that every new aspect of time and space, instead of shaking

our Faith, will give us a still deeper sense of security. The moon and the stars are only Your footprints. We are Your children forever and ever. Amen.

PRAYER FOR HELP
AT THE TIME OF DEATH

JOHN DONNE'S *celebrity as a poet in 17th century England is so widespread today that his vocation as a clergyman is frequently forgotten, although some of his best poems reflect the spirituality of his mature years. In his own day he was widely considered his nation's leading preacher and he was far better known for prayers like this one than for any of his poetry.*

ETERNAL and most glorious God, suffer me not so to undervalue myself as to give away soul—Thy soul, Thy dear and precious soul—for nothing; and all the world is nothing if the soul must be given for it. Preserve, therefore, my soul O Lord, because it belongs to Thee, and preserve my body because it belongs to my soul. Thou alone dost steer my boat through all its voyage, but has a more especial care of it when it comes to a narrow current, or to a dangerous fall of waters. Thou hast a care of the preservation of my body in all the ways of my life; but in the straits of death, open Thine eyes wider, and enlarge Thy providence towards me so far that no illness or agony may shake and benumb the soul. Do Thou so make my bed in all my sickness that, being used to Thy hand, I may be content with any bed of Thy making. Amen.

PRAYER ON NATIONAL HOLIDAYS

The following is adapted from a prayer by the REVEREND THEO-
DORE PARKER *on Washington's Birthday in 1857. The Reverend
Mr. Parker was celebrated for the power of his prayers, several
of which are included in this volume. Years later Louisa May
Alcott was to recall the first time she had heard him, writing:
"It was unlike any prayer I had ever heard; not cold and formal
as if uttered from a sense of duty, not a display of eloquence, nor
an impious directing of Diety in His duties toward humanity.
It was a quiet talk with God, as if long intercourse and much love
had made it natural and easy for the son to seek the Father."*

ATHER, we thank Thee for the great land in which we
live; we bless Thee for its favored situation, and its wide spread
from ocean to ocean, from lake to gulf. We thank Thee for the
millions of people who have grown up here in the midst of the
continent. We bless Thee for all the good institutions which are
established here; we thank Thee for whatsoever of justice is made
into law of the state, for all of piety, of loving-kindness and
tender mercy which are taught in many a various church and
practices by noble women and earnest men.

We bless Thee for our fathers, who in their day of small things
put their confidence in Thee, and went from one kingdom to
another people, few and strangers there, and at last, guided by a
religious star, came to this land and put up their prayers in
a wilderness. We thank Thee that the desert place has become a
garden, and the wild forest, full of beasts and prowling men, is
tenanted now with cities and beautiful with towns. We bless
Thee for the great men whom Thou gavest us at every period of
our nation's story; we thank Thee for such as were wise in coun-

cil, those also who were valiant in fight, and by whose right arm our redemption was wrought out.

We thank Thee for the unbounded wealth which has been gathered from our fields, or drawn from the sea, or digged from the bosom of the earth, and wrought out in our manifold places of toil throughout the land. We bless Thee for the schools which let light in on many a dark and barren place; and we thank Thee for noble and generous men and women in our own day who speak as they are moved by Thy holy spirit, and turn many into righteousness. So may Thy kingdom come and Thy will be done on earth as it is in heaven. Amen.

PRAYER FOR THE START OF
A NEW ENTERPRISE

CREATOR of the universe, by Whose will the world is renewed day by day, Thou hast implanted in us a spark of Thy creative spirit. Thou dost arouse us from lethargy and dost send us forth to work and to achieve. Thus are we impelled to seek improvement, to make new plans, to organize and to build. For this creative impulse, for the desire to progress, for the urge towards greater achievement, we thank Thee, O Creator. Thou hast made us partners of Thee in the building of the world.

Therefore I pray to Thee: guard Thou my steps in the new enterprise which I am about to begin. Grant that its success be not built upon the ruins of another's failure; that no added prosperity which may come to me will increase the misery of my fellowman.

Thine earth is bountiful. Thou openest Thy hand and satisfiest all with Thy favor. May, therefore, the achievement which I hope to attain for myself and my dear ones add also to the contentment of others. Let my work be done in harmony with Thy laws of justice, goodness and truth.

Strengthen me, O Lord, in the enterprise which I am now beginning. Make clear to my vision that I may discern the outlines of the future. Make strong my will that I may not falter when the tasks grow heavy. Make wise my judgment that I be not led into folly. More than for all these blessings, I pray, O Lord, that the strains of new work shall not injure my health, nor so absorb my energies that I neglect my dear ones, or become estranged from the worship of Thee. Let me walk in the light of Thy presence so that success will add to my spiritual strength and my achievement be a source of encouragement and blessing. Amen.

PRAYER FOR GUIDANCE

This prayer is by BISHOP PRINCE A. TAYLOR, JR., *Resident Bishop of the New Jersey Area, in the United Methodist Church.*

ETERNAL GOD OUR FATHER, Whose thoughts are beyond our comprehension and Whose ways are past finding out, we thank You for the glimpses of Your glory from day to day, and for the manifestations of Your love in the midst of our wretchedness and greed. You give us light in darkness, and make plain our pathway in the deserts of doubt and uncertainty. May this path become a highway to peace and understanding; and may the ageless yearning of man come to pass: "That the mountain of the house of the Lord be established, and all nations shall flow to it." Make us sensitive to our heritage and responsive to the challenges of our day. As we search to find new roads to the goal of our faith, show us where the roads begin. Free us from anxiety as we face the duties which lie before us and the difficulties still unknown.

We seek Your grace in these troubled times, that we may be instruments of Your peace and promoters of Your will. May we keep our purposes clear and our visions keen that we may face the responsibilities of this hour with high resolve. Give us courage equal to the task, wisdom to know Your will, and the forthrightness to do it. May we never feel so pushed by our problems that we cannot feel the pull of the stars. And make known in every human heart the Lordship of Your Son, our Savior, Jesus Christ our Lord. Amen.

PRAYER FOR REST

This prayer is by the REVEREND EDWARD B. PUSEY, *one of the outstanding theologians of the late 19th century, and a pillar of the High Church movement in England.*

ET ME not seek out of Thee what I can find only in Thee, O Lord: peace and rest and joy and bliss, which abide only in Thine abiding joy. Lift up my soul above the weary round of harassing thoughts to Thy eternal presence. Lift up my soul to the pure, bright, serene, radiant atmosphere of Thy presence, that there I may breathe freely, there repose in Thy love, there be at rest from myself, and from all things that weary me; and thence return, arrayed with Thy peace, to do and bear what shall please Thee. Amen.

[38]

PRAYER OF THANKSGIVING

WE GIVE THANKS unto Thee, for Thou art the Lord our God and the God of our fathers for ever and ever; Thou art the rock of our lives, the shield of our salvation through every generation. We will give thanks unto Thee and declare Thy praise for our lives which are committed unto Thy hand, and for Thy miracles, which are daily with us, and for Thy wonders and Thy benefits, which are wrought at all times, evening, morn and noon. O Thou Who art all good, Whose mercies fail not; Thou, merciful Being, Whose loving-kindnesses never cease, we have ever hoped in Thee. Amen.

PSALM 90

LORD, Thou hast been our dwelling place in all generations.

Before the mountains were brought forth, or ever Thou hadst formed the earth and the world, even from everlasting to everlasting, Thou art God.

Thou turnest man to destruction; and sayest, Return, ye children of men.

For a thousand years in Thy sight are but as yesterday when it is past, and as a watch in the night.

Thou carriest them away as with a flood; they are as a sleep: in the morning they are like grass which groweth up.

In the morning it flourisheth, and groweth up; in the evening it is cut down, and withereth.

For we are consumed by Thine anger, and by Thy wrath are we troubled. Thou hast set our iniquities before Thee, our secret sins in the light of Thy countenance.

[39]

For all our days are passed away in Thy wrath: we spend our years as a tale that is told.

The days of our years are threescore years and ten; and if by reason of strength they be fourscore years, yet is their strength labor and sorrow; for it is soon cut off, and we fly away.

Who knoweth the power of Thine anger? Even according to Thy fear, so is Thy wrath.

So teach us to number our days, that we may apply our hearts unto wisdom.

Return, O Lord, how long? And let it repent Thee concerning Thy servants.

O satisfy us early with Thy mercy; that we may rejoice and be glad all our days.

Make us glad according to the days wherein Thou hast afflicted us, and the years wherein we have seen evil.

Let Thy work appear unto Thy servants, and Thy glory unto their children.

And let the beauty of the Lord our God be upon us; and establish Thou the work of our hands upon us; yea, the work of our hands establish Thou it.

PRAYER FOR
FRUITFUL SEASONS

ALMIGHTY GOD, Who hast blessed the earth that it should be fruitful and bring forth whatsoever is needful for the life of man, and hast commanded us to work with quietness, and eat our own bread; bless the labors of the husbandman, and grant such seasonable weather that we may gather in the fruits of the earth, and ever rejoice in Thy goodness, to the praise of Thy holy Name; through Jesus Christ our Lord. Amen.

PRAYER FOR RAIN

O GOD, heavenly Father, Who by Thy Son Jesus Christ hast promised to all those who seek Thy kingdom, and the righteousness thereof, all things necessary to their bodily sustenance; send us, we beseech Thee, in this our necessity, such moderate rain and showers, that we may receive the fruits of the earth to our comfort, and to Thy honor; through Jesus Christ our Lord. Amen.

THANKSGIVING FOR RAIN

O GOD, our heavenly Father, by Whose gracious providence the former and the latter rain descend upon the earth, that it may bring forth fruit for the use of man; we give Thee humble thanks that it hath pleased Thee to send us rain to our great comfort, and to the glory of Thy holy Name; through Jesus Christ our Lord. Amen.

PRAYER OF PENITENCE

THOU favorest man with knowledge, and teachest mortals understanding. O favor us with knowledge, understanding and discernment from Thee. Blessed art Thou, O Lord, gracious giver of knowledge.

Cause us to return, O our Father, unto Thy law; draw us near, O our King, unto Thy service, and bring us back in perfect repentance unto Thy presence. Blessed art Thou, O Lord, Who delightest in repentance.

Forgive us, O our Father, for we have sinned; pardon us, O our King, for we have transgressed; for Thou dost pardon and forgive. Blessed art Thou, O Lord, Who are gracious, and dost abundantly forgive.

Look upon our affliction and plead our cause, and redeem us speedily for Thy Name's sake; for Thou art a mighty redeemer. Blessed art Thou, O Lord, the Redeemer of Israel.

PRAYER IN SPRING-TIME

The Reverend Doctor Donald M. Meisel *submitted this prayer for* Treasured Volume. *As Minister of The First Presbyterian Church in Princeton, New Jersey, the Reverend Doctor Meisel graces a pulpit which dates back to pre-Revolutionary days.*

God of hope, short of being able to hope in Thee we look on a majestic day such as this with a twinge of sadness. We sense that such beauty is out of keeping with so much tragedy and uncertainty and waste in the world around us. But as sons of Thine, sons of hope, we see in the forsythia, the magnolia, and the cherry tree signs of the promise of a world that is yet to be.

O God of hope, short of being able to hope in Thee we cannot turn our gaze from war and brutality and the hardware of brutality, from man's inhumanity to man. Only with Thine eyes can we discover the flower growing out of the crumbling wall. Only by Thee can we discern the acts of kindness and sensitivity and

[42]

caring and dare to believe that here are the seeds of the Kingdom, the real signs of the future.

O God of hope, be with those for whom hope is an especially precious and scarce commodity, those whose present state is anything but the realization of past hopes. Be with them as we think of them now and give them that ability to live beyond their own limitations which we marvel to see in others from time to time and which we covet for those whom we name.

O God of hope, help us to act on our hopes, to bring the power and the promise of the future into the troubled spots of the present age.

O Thou who didst invest Thyself in us, help us to invest ourselves in the coming of Thy Kingdom. And hear us now as we pray the prayer that Jesus taught us to pray. Amen.

PRAYER TO AID OTHERS TO SUBMIT TO GOD'S WILL

It is frequently difficult to distinguish between the poems and the prayers of CHRISTINA GEORGINA ROSETTI, *the 19th century English poet. A devout High Church woman, her poetry is full of prayer and her devotional works, such as this, reflect her poetic touch.*

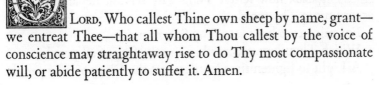 LORD, Who callest Thine own sheep by name, grant—we entreat Thee—that all whom Thou callest by the voice of conscience may straightaway rise to do Thy most compassionate will, or abide patiently to suffer it. Amen.

[43]

PRAYER FOR A
PERSON UNDER AFFLICTION

MERCIFUL GOD, and heavenly Father, Who hast taught us in Thy holy word that Thou dost not willingly afflict or grieve the children of men; look with pity, we beseech Thee, upon the sorrows of Thy servant for whom our prayers are offered. Remember him/her, O Lord, in mercy; endue his/her soul with patience; comfort him/her with a sense of Thy goodness; lift up Thy countenance upon him/her, and give him/her peace; through Jesus Christ our Lord. Amen.

SIMEON'S PRAYER

According to Luke ii, 25–28, Simeon was a just man who was in the Temple in Jerusalem when Mary and Joseph brought the infant Jesus there for circumcision and the Holy Spirit inspired Simeon, who took the infant in his arms and (Luke ii, 29–32) spoke the words which have long been a recognition and submission—of and to God's will.

LORD, now lettest Thou Thy servant depart in peace, according to Thy word:
   For mine eyes have seen Thy Salvation,
   Which Thou hast prepared before the face of all people;
   A Light to lighten the Gentiles, and the Glory of Thy people Israel.

GENERAL PRAYER

IVE US understanding, O Lord our God, to know Thy ways; open our hearts to fear Thee, and forgive us so that we may be redeemed. Keep us far from sorrow; satiate us on the pastures of Thy land, and gather our scattered ones from the far corners of the earth. Let them that go astray be judged according to Thy will, and wave Thy hand over the wicked. Let the righteous rejoice in the rebuilding of Thy city and in the establishment of Thy temple, and in the flourishing of the horn of David, Thy servant, and in the clear shining light of the son of Jesse, Thine anointed. Even before we call, do Thou answer. Blessed art Thou, O Lord, Who hearkenest unto prayer. Amen.

PRAYER IN
A HOUSE OF MOURNING

E ARE assembled with our friends in the shadow that has fallen on their home. We raise our voices together in prayer to the Father above, asking for comfort and strength. We need light when gloom darkens our home; whence can it come but from the Creator of light? We need fortitude and resignation under the chastening of the Lord; whence can these come save from Him who lays the burden upon us? Who among us has not passed through trials and bereavements! Some bear fresh wounds in their hearts and therefore feel the more keenly the kinship of sorrow. Others whose days of mourning are remote, still recall the comfort that sympathy brought to their sorrowing

[45]

hearts. And those of us who have not yet tasted of the bitter cup cannot know how soon we may be called on to drink it. All that we prize is but lent to us and we must surrender it when God demands. We are travelers on the same road which leads to the same end.

Eternal is Thy power, O Lord, Thou art mighty to save. In loving-kindness Thou sustainest the living; in the multitude of Thy mercies, Thou preservest all. Thou upholdest the falling and healest the sick, freest the captives, and keepest faith with Thy children in death as in life. Who is like unto Thee, Almighty God, author of life and death, source of salvation? Praised be Thou, O Lord, Who hast implanted within us eternal life. Amen.

MOURNERS' PRAYER

XTOLLED and hallowed be the name of God throughout the world which He has created, and which He governs according to His righteous will. Just is He in all His ways, and wise are all His decrees. May His kingdom come, and His will be done in all the earth.

Blessed be the Lord of life, the righteous Judge for evermore.

To the departed whom we now remember, may peace and bliss be granted in the world of eternal life. There may they find grace and mercy before the Lord of heaven and earth. May their souls rejoice in that ineffable good which God has laid up for those that fear Him, and may their memory be a blessing unto those that cherish it.

May the Father of peace send peace to all troubled souls, and comfort all the bereaved among us. Amen.

MEMORIAL DAY PRAYER

LMIGHTY GOD, our heavenly Father, in Whose hands
are the living and the dead; we give Thee thanks for all those
Thy servants who have laid down their lives in the service of our
country. Grant to them Thy mercy and the light of Thy presence,
that the good work which Thou hast begun in them may be
perfected; through Jesus Christ Thy Son our Lord. Amen.

PRAYER ON
VISITING A CEMETERY

HE LORD is nigh unto the broken in heart. He saveth
them that are of contrite spirit. Many are the afflictions of the
righteous, yet the Lord delivereth him out of them all.

The Lord redeemeth the soul of His servants, none shall be
condemned that trust in Him.

O eternal Father, Thou keepest faith with Thy children in
death as in life. Thou dost grant us the privilege of living in the
service of Thee and dost bestow upon us eternal peace when our
toils on earth are ended. I thank Thee for the blessed life of my
loved one who has here been laid to rest. For the joy of companionship, for the plans and achievements and even the shared
disappointments, for all of them I humbly praise Thy name.

I come now to pay homage to this beloved memory. Grant to
my dear one eternal peace and may he/she be a light unto my
path and a blessing day by day. Amen.

PRAYER AT THE GRAVE OF A RELATIVE

I STAND by the grave of my dear . . . . . . , feeling the burden of the last parting on earth; and I would lift up my heart in prayer unto Thee, O God, Who givest life and takest it away.

I thank Thee, O God, for the ties that united my . . . . . . and me in life; for the watchful interest in my welfare, the ready sympathy, and the many deeds of loving-kindness which bound our souls with the lasting cords of family love.

Now, O God, that Thou, in Thine infinite justice and wisdom hast called my dear . . . . . . hence, I cherish these memories; and I think of the departed soul as in Thy keeping among the righteous.

Though the bonds of affection are severed, yet strong as death is the devotion of my heart. And in this hour, at this grave, I would renew the sweet sentiments that bound us in life, and dedicate them unto the service of my fellow men. May Thy peace, O God, abide with us in life and in death. Amen.

PRAYER FOR THE POOR

O THOU Who art love, and Who seest all the suffering, injustice and misery which reign in this world, have pity, we implore Thee, on the work of Thy hands. Look mercifully upon the poor, the oppressed, and all who are heavy laden with error, labor, and sorrow. Fill our hearts with deep compassion for those who suffer, and hasten the coming of Thy kingdom of justice and truth. Amen.

PRAYER
FOR THE TROUBLED

LMIGHTY GOD, the refuge of all that are distressed, grant unto us that, in all trouble of this our mortal life, we may flee to the knowledge of Thy loving-kindness and tender mercy; that so, sheltering ourselves therein, the storms of life may pass over us, and not shake the peace of God that is within us. Whatsoever this life may bring us, grant that it may never take from us the full faith that Thou art our Father. Grant us Thy light, that we may have life, through Jesus Christ our Lord. Amen.

MORNING PRAYER

LESSED art Thou, O Lord our God,
King of the universe.

O lead us not into the power of sin, or of transgression or iniquity, or of temptation, or of scorn: let not the evil inclination have sway over us: keep us far from a bad man and a bad companion: make us cleave to the good inclination and to good works: subdue our inclination so that it may submit itself unto Thee; and let us obtain this day, and every day, grace, favor and mercy in Thine eyes, and in the eyes of all who behold us; and bestow loving-kindnesses upon us. Blessed art Thou, O Lord, Who bestowest loving-kindnesses upon Thy people Israel.

It is our duty to thank, praise and glorify Thee, to bless, to sanctify and to offer praise and thanksgiving unto Thy Name. Happy are we! how goodly is our portion, and how pleasant is our lot, and how beautiful our heritage! Happy are we who,

early and late, morning and evening, twice every day, declare:
Hear, O Israel: the Lord our God, the Lord is One. Blessed be
His name, Whose glorious kingdom is for ever and ever. Amen.

NIGHT PRAYER

This comes from the 9th century pen of ALCUIN, *a theologian
and pioneering educator. Alcuin was a friend and adviser of
Charlemagne.*

LMIGHTY and merciful God, the fountain of all goodness, Who knowest the thoughts of our hearts, we confess unto
Thee that we have sinned against Thee, and done evil in Thy
sight. Wash us, we beseech Thee, from the stains of our past
sins, and give us grace and power to put away all hurtful things;
so that, being delivered from the bondage of sin, we may bring
forth worthy fruits of repentance.

O eternal Light, shine into our hearts. O eternal Goodness,
deliver us from evil. O eternal Power, be Thou our support.
Eternal Wisdom, scatter the darkness of our ignorance. Eternal
Pity, have mercy upon us. Grant unto us that with all our hearts,
and minds, and strength, we may evermore seek Thy face; and
finally bring us, in Thine infinite mercy, to Thy holy presence.
So strengthen our weakness that, following in the footsteps of
Thy blessed Son, we may obtain Thy mercy, and enter into Thy
promised joy. Amen.

PRAYER FOR TRUE CHARITY

LORD, Thy charity never faileth. Touch the hearts of men with humanity, that they may learn justice and to love their brothers. Make us nobler, and braver and holier. Teach us to love all men. So let us be Thy children, loving those that hate us, and praying for such as despitefully use us. So may Thy kingdom come, and Thy will be done on earth as it is in heaven. Amen.

MIGHTY AND RIGHTEOUS FATHER

The Bishop of the Illinois Area of the United Methodist Church, BISHOP LANCE WEBB, *wrote this reflection on the glory of God.*

UR MIGHTY and righteous Father, you are ruling our universe in the Heaven of fullest reality. In Your love You call us to a new life through a servant church in a world on fire. We thank You for the great light shining in the face of Jesus Christ through Whom we begin to see not only Your loving glory in all creation, but also the glory of Your purpose even within our little selves—yes, even in the threatening and tragic divisions and distresses of our world.

Grant us this hour a new vision of your purpose for us—the infinite possibilities still to be fulfilled in each of us and in all mankind—so that we may not only have the power to reach the moon but also the more difficult achievement of reaching the place of peace and cooperation which is Your will for all mankind.

Help us not to think either too little or too much of ourselves,

[51]

that in the transfiguration of man in our scientific achievements we lose not sight of the needed transformation of our humanity by Your spiritual recreation.

Forgive us, O merciful Father, that we have so often neglected or ignored Your light and sought to create a luster of our own. We confess before You our share in the guilty suffering of our fellow man, not only the things we have done but also that we might have done had we understood and obeyed Your truth.

O Lord of the farthest star and of the smallest child, forgive us and help us to surrender our shells, the false world of illusion we have built around us. Dig us out of the selfishness and pride behind which we have hidden from You and rationalized and justified our sins and failures against our brothers and our own true selves.

In Your blazing presence may we begin to see the dawn of a new day, a new life, a new courage, a new power to love and to give that which is eternally worth giving—the vision and acceptance of Your kingdom of love which unites us as one family and saves us from the kingdom of loveless hell.

Minister now to hearts that are weary and sad, discouraged with self-pity and grief. Bring Your healing into all of our hearts that we may be restored to our true destiny. We pray not for ourselves alone, but for all who are hungry and defeated. We pray for Your judgment to be revealed to all of us, and Your justice to be sought by the leaders of the nations. Grant to them and to each of us the sensitive spirit and the willing heart to see and do all we can in our own spheres to right the wrongs and to accept Your peace.

May we in quietness and confidence possess our souls in the knowledge that you are ruling still in all this vast universe and may we, no matter what others do, accept Your rule and the joy of hope and the freedom to love that results in our own lives, through Jesus Christ our Lord. Amen.

PRAYER FOR GRACE
TO SPEND OUR TIME WELL

This prayer is by the RIGHT REVEREND JEREMY TAYLOR, *Episcopal Bishop of Down and Connor in northern Ireland in the 17th century. His devotional works are marked by deep piety, and—although his sermons are regarded by some as among the greatest in the English language—he inveighed against the "impertinent and ignorant . . . who think all religion is a sermon."*

ETERNAL GOD Who from all eternity dost behold and love Thy own glories and perfections infinite, and hast created me to do the word of God, after the manner of men, and to serve Thee in this generation, and according to my capacities; give me Thy grace, that I may be a curious and prudent spender of my time, so as I may best prevent or resist all temptation, and be profitable to the Christian commonwealth, and by discharging all my duty may glorify Thy Name. Take from me all slothfulness, and give me a diligent and an active spirit, and wisdom to choose my employment, that I may do works proportionable to my person, and to the dignity of a Christian, and may fill up all the spaces of my time with actions of religion and charity, that when the devil assaults me, he may not find me idle: and my dearest Lord, at His sudden coming, may find me busy in lawful, necessary, and pious actions, improving my talent entrusted to me by Thee, my Lord, that I may enter into the joy of my Lord to partake of His eternal felicities, even for Thy mercy's sake and for my dearest Savior's sake. Amen.

TO THE PROPRE ANGELL

This is one of the earliest prayers printed in the English language. It is selected from The Fifteen O's and Other Prayers, *one of the eighty books printed by William Caxton, the first English printer. It was printed in the late 15th century "by order of Princess Elizabeth, Queen of England and of France, and also of Princess Margaret, Mother of our Sovereign Lord the King." The fifteen then-familiar prayers referred to in the title all began with the invocation "O," as in "O blessed . . ." Even when printed in the more legible type of today, the spelling and punctuation of Caxton makes most of the prayers difficult to follow. With slight modifications this prayer to guardian angels is probably the plainest. Caxton spelled "thee" with only three letters: "the"; and—here, at least—"no" in three letters: "noo"; "ghostly" is spelled "goostly." A slanting stroke, like the virgule (/), was used for different punctuation marks and it has been left here as it occurs in the original. However, I have spelled out "thee," dropped one phrase, and added two commas in the following adaptation.*

GLORYOUS angell to whom our Blessed Lord of His most merciful grace hath taken me to kepe. To thee, I sinful creature crye and call . . . / beseeching thee ever to be singular comforte to me in all my nede/ Suffer me never to be overcome with temptacyon or synfull dede/ But helpe me that by grace I may ever in vertuous livynge procede/ At the hour of my deth present that my goostly enemy in me have noo power/ and after, brynge me to blisse/ Where ever I may live and prayse our Savyour. Amen/

PRAISE AND SUPPLICATION

This prayer is from the REVEREND DOCTOR GEORGE E. SWEAZEY, *Minister of the Webster Groves Presbyterian Church, in Webster Groves, Missouri, and Moderator of the 181st General Assembly of the United Presbyterian Church of the U. S. A.*

ALMIGHTY GOD, by Whose ancient law the stars swing on their courses, by Whose vitality life has thrust out and unfolded on this earth, by Whose inspiration scholars have searched for truth, prophets have spoken and poets dreamed, and by Whose call I have been stirred to see Thee now—save me from the sacrilege of having a little God in a box, a private graven image, a puppet God Whom I can manipulate to suit my purposes.

How great Thou art! Thou art mighty beyond all men's imagining, wise beyond what wisdom means, loving beyond any concept there has been of love. But I praise Thee that, with all Thine incomprehensible range and splendor, Thou hast graciously come within men's comprehension so that they can, in limits but still truly, know and worship Thee. In Thy mercy Thou didst humble Thyself, to be revealed on earth through Jesus Christ. In Him I find Thee in terms which I can understand. Through Him Thou dost speak to me in my vocabulary.

So today, O God, I dare to bring before Thee my little problems and concerns, my longings and my needs. The God revealed in the face of Jesus Christ is a God Who knows and cares about me. Such knowledge is too wonderful for me! I can only, in awed gratitude, accept it with full confidence and trust.

Make the most mundane affairs of every day radiant with Thy presence. Show me the splendor in the work I have to do. Help me to see Thee in the dear people whom I am meeting every day. Fill my life with the practical acts of kindness and the evident love for others through which I can express my worship and my love of Thee. Come from Thy cosmic mysteries and go with me on my daily walk. Through Jesus Christ. Amen.

JESUS, LOVER OF MY SOUL

The REVEREND CHARLES WESLEY, *younger brother of the father of Methodism, is said to have written more than one thousand hymns. This is one of the best known. Another—lesser known— is the Hymn for New Year's Day, included toward the end of this* Treasured Volume.

JESUS, lover of my soul,
Let me to Thy bosom fly,
While the nearer waters roll,
While the tempest still is high;
Hide me, O my Savior! hide,
Till the storm of life be past;
Safe into the haven guide;
Oh! receive my soul at last!

Other refuge have I none;
Hangs my helpless soul on Thee;
Leave, ah! leave me not alone,
Still support and comfort me!
All my trust on Thee is stayed,
All my help from Thee I bring;
Cover my defenceless head
With the shadow of Thy wing!

HEAR, O ISRAEL

EAR, O ISRAEL: the Lord our God, the Lord is One. Praised be His Name Whose glorious kingdom is forever and ever. Amen.

PRAYER FOR THE GRACE TO FACE PROBLEMS

This selection is by the REVEREND DOCTOR JOHN COVENTRY SMITH, *General Secretary of the Commission on Ecumenical Mission and Relations of the United Presbyterian Church in the United States of America.*

UR FATHER: we come to You today disturbed by the world. There is pain, there is sorrow, there is poverty, there is cruelty, there is suffering, there is war. We confess that we try to ignore these things but we are here because we cannot ignore them.

Help us to know why we are in the world. We know You have created the world and us. And, You have not left us alone.

We thank You that Jesus was born, that He is a human being with all the temptations and troubles of a man in a human society. We thank You that He shared with us the knowledge of being sent by You into the world, that in this Jesus there is the very nature of Your own spirit and person.

Help us to know that we are to be like Christ, that He said, "As the Father has sent Me, so send I you."

We have long tried to be like Christ, and we have so often

failed. Once more we ask for forgiveness. This time we ask also for Your strength. Help us to share the suffering and the joy of people in our world. Help us to do what we can to heal the wounds and establish justice. Help us to know and confess that we are part of the problem of the world, its pain and suffering reflect the results of our own selfishness and indifference.

Teach us that being like Christ is costly—that we may have to sacrifice some friendships, the esteem of our neighbors, even our material security. Remind us that Jesus did that—it cost Him His life. Make us willing to be like Him.

Give us a new vision of Your kingdom—the kingdom You will establish but which begins here and now. Make us a part of it. Help us to know this foretaste of Your promise for all of mankind, that Your reign begins with us in all our relationships of family and neighborhood and nation and world.

Through Jesus Christ, our fellow human being and divine Lord. Amen.

HYMN TO GOD

In a letter to Thomas Jefferson, JOHN ADAMS, *second president of the United States, gave this brief prayer as his favorite. It was written by a Greek philosopher of the third century before Christ, Cleanthes. It demonstrates how even a pagan, if thoughtful, recognizes the sovereignty of God. Adams quoted it in Greek, but gave grudging approval to the translation by Alexander Pope which is used here.*

FATHER of all! in every age,
In every clime adored
By saint, by savage and by sage—
Jehovah, Jove or Lord.

BRIDE'S PRAYER

To Thee, O God, I open my heart in prayer and thanksgiving. I rejoice in the love that has come to me to enrich my life. Thou hast blessed me with the devotion of a man who shall be my lifelong friend and companion. In all the vicissitudes of my life, I look to Thee for light and support, for help and guidance.

Be with me, O Father, as I strive to fulfill the manifold tasks of a true and devoted wife. May I learn to realize that more precious and enduring than grace and beauty are the tender words we speak and the kindly acts we do. Fill me with the spirit of the faithful daughters in Israel, who by their wisdom and virtue won the love, admiration and confidence of their husbands and children. Make me worthy of Thy blessings, and help me to build my home on the lasting foundations of love and truth and peace. Amen.

BRIDEGROOM'S PRAYER

Almighty God and Father, as I am about to enter into the bond of wedlock, I pray for Thy light and Thy blessing. Open my eyes to see that the love in my heart is a gift from Thy hand, to increase my happiness and to add worth and significance to my life. Help me to fulfill all the duties of my new life. May I always be worthy of the trust and devotion of my beloved. May I always be to her a faithful husband, a true friend and protector.

Let Thy blessing rest upon the home we shall establish together. May it be a home where love and peace, mutual forbearance and devotion shall always abide. May the spirit of religion ever pervade its atmosphere. Give me the vision to see that without Thy presence to sustain and comfort us we shall fail to fulfill the divine plan of our lives.

May ours be a union of hands for honest toil and fruitful effort. May we work and strive together through days of joy and sorrow, to achieve the happiness for which our hearts are yearning. Amen.

BLESSING FOR
A MARRIAGE RING

LMIGHTY GOD, we beseech Thee to sanctify and hallow this ring, and grant that he who gives it and she who receives it, may live for each other, and both for Thee: through Jesus Christ our Lord. Amen.

A WEDDING
ANNIVERSARY PRAYER

THOU Who has blessed our fathers of old, bestow Thy blessings upon ...... and .... Cause them to prosper in the way of life which they shall pursue, sharing with one another life's trials as well as life's joys, and thereby finding grace in the eyes of all who see them. Aid them to build a home that shall honor the house of Israel. May peace ever dwell within their home; contentment, love and joy within their hearts. May they grow old together in health and be ever grateful unto Thee for their union. Amen.

[60]

PRAYER FOR SILVER OR GOLDEN
WEDDING ANNIVERSARY

ᴇᴛᴇʀɴᴀʟ Gᴏᴅ and Father! In the fullness of this day's joy, we turn our hearts in praise and gratitude to Thee. We thank Thee for Thy favor which has preserved and sustained this happy couple and permitted them to reach this hour. In the midst of family (and friends) and loved ones, they look back in reverent and grateful reminiscence upon the stretch of years since first they pledged their hearts to one another and to Thee. Many and varied have been the experiences since that hour; many have been the mingled occasions of victory and defeat, of fulfillment and disappointment. We thank Thee for the joys unnumbered with which Thou hast sweetened their lives; and likewise, we praise Thee for the trials which, with Thy help, they have surmounted. Our times are in Thy hand; we know that Thou wilt guide and sustain us even unto the end. As Thou hast blessed them in the past, so continue to bless them in the years to come. May it be Thy will that these be years of health and contentment; of unclouded bliss in the circle of their family and loved ones; of mutual and unbroken service of righteousness, love and peace to those who are far and to those who are near. Amen.

GENERAL PETITION

Lᴏʀᴅ Jᴇsᴜs Cʜʀɪsᴛ, Who saidst unto Thine apostles, peace I leave with you, My peace I give unto you; regard not our sins, but the faith of Thy church; and grant to it that peace and unity which is according to Thy will, Who livest and reignest with the Father and the Holy Ghost, one God, world without end. Amen.

Assist us mercifully, O Lord, in these our supplications and prayers, and dispose the way of Thy servants towards the attainment of everlasting salvation; that, among all the changes and chances of this mortal life, they may ever be defended by Thy most gracious and ready help; through Jesus Christ our Lord. Amen.

Direct us, O Lord, in all our doings, with Thy most gracious favor, and further us with Thy continual help; that in all our works begun, continued, and ended in Thee, we may glorify Thy holy Name, and finally, by Thy mercy, obtain everlasting life; through Jesus Christ our Lord. Amen.

PRAYER OF THE GREAT HOURS

No collection of great prayers could be complete without a representation of the Eastern Churches. The MOST REVEREND IAKOVOS, *Archbishop of the Greek Orthodox Church of North and South America, has submitted the following prayer from the Service of the Great Hours.*

HOU WHO at all times, and at every hour, both in heaven and on earth, art worshipped and glorified, O Christ, our God, long-suffering and plenteous in mercy and compassion; Who lovest the just and showest mercy to those who are hardened in sin; Who callest all men to salvation through the promise of good things to come; do Thou, the same Lord, receive also our supplications at this present time, and direct our lives according to Thy commandments. Sanctify our souls; purify our bodies;

set aright our minds; cleanse our thoughts; and deliver us from all calamity, wrath and distress. Compass us round about with Thy holy angels; that, guided and guarded by their host, we may attain unto the unity of the faith, and unto the comprehension of Thine ineffable glory. For blessed art Thou unto ages of ages. Amen.

PSALM 71

A psalm for the elderly

IN THEE, O Lord, do I put my trust: let me never be put to confusion.

Deliver me in Thy righteousness, and cause me to escape: incline Thine ear unto me, and save me.

Be Thou my strong habitation, whereunto I may continually resort: Thou hast given commandment to save me; for Thou art my rock and my fortress.

Deliver me, O my God, out of the hand of the wicked, out of the hand of the unrighteous and cruel man.

For Thou art my hope, O Lord God: Thou art my trust from my youth.

By Thee have I been holden up from the womb: Thou art He that took me out of my mother's bowels: my praise shall be continually of Thee.

I am as a wonder unto many; but Thou art my strong refuge.

Let my mouth be filled with Thy praise and with Thy honor all the day.

Cast me not off in the time of old age; forsake me not when my strength faileth.

For mine enemies speak against me; and they that lay wait for my soul take counsel together,

Saying, God hath forsaken him: persecute and take him; for there is none to deliver him.

O God, be not far from me: O my God, make haste for my help.

Let them be confounded and consumed that are adversaries to my soul; let them be covered with reproach and dishonor that seek my hurt.

But I will hope continually, and will yet praise Thee more and more.

My mouth shall show forth Thy righteousness and Thy salvation all the day; for I know not the numbers thereof.

I will go in the strength of the Lord God: I will make mention of Thy righteousness, even of Thine only.

O God, Thou hast taught me from my youth: and hitherto have I declared Thy wondrous works.

Now also when I am old and gray-headed, O God, forsake me not; until I have showed Thy strength unto this generation, and Thy power to every one that is to come.

Thy righteousness also, O God, is very high, Who hast done great things: O God, who is like unto Thee!

Thou, which hast showed me great and sore troubles, shalt quicken me again, and shalt bring me up again from the depths of the earth.

Thou shalt increase my greatness, and comfort me on every side.

I will also praise Thee with the psaltery, even Thy truth, O my God: unto Thee will I sing with the harp, O Thou Holy One of Israel.

My lips shall greatly rejoice when I sing unto Thee, and my soul, which Thou hast redeemed.

My tongue also shall talk of Thy righteousness all the day long: for they are confounded, for they are brought unto shame, that seek my hurt.

GRADUATION
DAY PRAYER

This prayer is by the REVEREND DOCTOR NATHAN A. PERILMAN, *Senior Rabbi of Congregation Emanu-El in New York City, the largest Jewish congregation in the world.*

EAVENLY FATHER: how good and how pleasant it is to be in the company of the learned and the wise; to sit for a time with great teachers and promising scholars who today receive their well-merited accolades after years of faithful and dedicated study. Man's surest salvation is in finding the light of knowledge —his greatest joy and hope in the pursuit and search thereof.

We proclaim our faith in this even today when so many students revile teachers, when they put the torch to books, when not knowing what they want or need to know they insist on charting the course of learning.

Be Thou with those whom we delight to see honored today. Grant that very soon they will be working in a quieter, less troubled world. Keep their courage high that they may not lose heart in the noblest of all callings—lighting candles for the dark, teaching understanding where there is confusion of mind, evoking reason and high purpose where there is only rage.

Hasten the day when once again great books and learned men will be honored by all Thy children everywhere. Only thus shall we find the way to share with Thee mastery of our universe. Only thus shall we establish peace among nations and peace with ourselves and our neighbors. Amen.

MARY, QUEEN OF SCOTS' PRAYER

This prayer of MARY, QUEEN OF SCOTS, *was written in her personal book of devotion just before her execution.*

O MASTER and Maker! my hope is in Thee,
My Jesus dear Savior! now set my soul free.
From this my hard prison, my spirit uprisen,
    Soars upward to Thee.
Thus moaning and groaning and bending the knee
I adore and implore that Thou liberate me.

PRAYER FOR PRISONERS

O GOD, let the sighing of the prisoner come before Thee, and mercifully grant unto us that we may be delivered by Thine almighty power from all bonds and chains of sin whether in our bodies or in our souls, through Jesus Christ Our Lord. Amen.

O LORD, forgive what I have been, sanctify what I am; and order what I shall be. Amen.

PRAYER FOR THE SICK

LESSED art Thou, O Lord,
Who answerest in time of trouble.

Heal us, O Lord, and we shall be healed; save us and we shall be saved; for Thou art our praise. Grant a perfect healing to all our wounds; may it be Thy will, O Lord our God, and God of our fathers, speedily to send a perfect healing from heaven, a healing of soul and body unto the sick . . . . . . , among the other sick of Israel; for Thou, almighty King, art a faithful and merciful Physician. Blessed art Thou, O Lord, Who healest the sick of Thy people Israel. Amen.

MORNING PRAYER

ROBERT LOUIS STEVENSON *was more than the "Teller of Tales"— as his neighbors in Samoa called him. Though no churchman, this master of English writing turned his great talents to the composition of a number of prayers, of which this is one, as is the Evening Prayer which follows it.*

HE DAY returns and brings us the petty round of irritating concerns and duties. Help us to play the man, help us to perform them with laughter and kind faces, let cheerfulness abound with industry. Give us to go blithely on our business all this day, bring us to our resting beds weary and content and undishonored, and grant us in the end the gift of sleep. Amen.

[67]

EVENING PRAYER

E BESEECH THEE, Lord to behold us with favor, folk of many families and nations gathered together in the peace of this roof, weak men and women subsisting under the covert of Thy patience. Be patient still; suffer us yet a while longer—with our broken purposes of good, with our idle endeavors against evil, suffer us a while longer to endure and (if it may be) help us to do better. Bless to us our extraordinary mercies; if the day come when these must be taken, brace us to play the man under affliction. Be with our friends, be with ourselves. Go with each of us to rest; if any awake, temper to them the dark hours of watching; and when the day returns, return to us, our Sun and Comforter, and call us up with morning faces and with morning hearts—eager to labor—eager to be happy, if happiness shall be our portion—and if the day be marked for sorrow, strong to endure it. Amen.

PRAYER FOR MORE PERFECT LOVE

GOD, perfect us in love, that we may conquer all selfishness and hatred of others; fill our hearts with Thy joy, and shed abroad in them Thy peace which passeth understanding; that those murmurings and disputing to which we are too prone may be overcome. Make us long-suffering and gentle, and thus subdue our hastiness and angry tempers, and grant that we may bring forth the blessed fruits of the Spirit, to Thy praise and glory, through Jesus Christ our Lord. Amen.

PRAYER FOR THE
BROTHERHOOD OF MAN

*Marble Collegiate Church in Manhattan was founded in 1628,
making it one of the oldest congregations in the nation. Its present minister, the* REVEREND DOCTOR NORMAN VINCENT PEALE,
*through his books, articles, broadcasts and lectures, has become
one of the best known churchmen in the country. It is from
Doctor Peale that we have this prayer.*

DEAR LORD, there are many things for which we want to
pray; things like health, and strength, and loved ones, and
friends, and for our daily bread. But there is one infinitely greater
prayer that we would offer to Thee, humbly beseeching that
Thou wouldst grant it.

We pray for love to fill the hearts of men, that in this world
we shall at last attain brotherhood and peace. Only Thou, O
Lord, working in the hearts of men, can establish love among
Thy children, and with it understanding. Amen.

A GENERAL PRAYER FOR
DISTRESSED NEIGHBORS

GOD, the Creator and Preserver of all mankind, we
humbly beseech Thee for all sorts and conditions of men; that
Thou wouldst be pleased to make Thy ways known unto them,

Thy saving health unto all nations. More especially we pray for Thy holy church universal; that it may be so guided and governed by Thy good Spirit, that all who profess and call themselves Christians may be led into the way of truth, and hold the faith in unity of spirit, in the bond of peace, and in righteousness of life. Finally, we commend to Thy fatherly goodness all those who are in any way afflicted, or distressed, in mind, body, or estate; especially ...... and ...... that it may please Thee to comfort and relieve them, according to their several necessities; giving them patience under their sufferings, and a happy issue out of all their afflictions. And this we beg for Jesus Christ's sake. Amen.

PRAYER OF SAINT FRANCIS

The SAINT FRANCIS *to whom this prayer is attributed is the widely venerated "little poor man of Assisi," the monk whose zeal for the service of God led him even into the fields to preach to the birds the glories of their Creator.*

ORD, make me an instrument of Thy peace. Where there is hatred, let me sow love; where there is injury, pardon; where there is doubt, faith; where there is despair, hope; where there is darkness, light; and where there is sickness, joy.

O Divine Master, grant that I may not so much seek to be consoled as to console; to be understood as to understand; to be loved as to love; for it is in giving that we receive; it is in pardoning that we are pardoned; and it is in dying that we are born to eternal life. Amen.

[70]

PRAYER FOR FRIENDS

BLESSED LORD, Who hast commanded us to love one another, grant us grace that, having received Thine undeserved bounty, we may love every one in Thee and for Thee. We implore Thy clemency for all; but especially for the friends whom Thy love has given to us. Love Thou them, O Thou fountain of love, and make them to love Thee with all their heart, that they may will and speak, and do those things only which are pleasing to Thee. Amen.

WE COME TO THEE, FATHER

From the REVEREND DOCTOR EDWIN H. TULLER, *General Secretary of the American Baptist Convention, we have this prayer for those who seek some refuge from the concerns of the day.*

E COME to Thee, our heavenly Father, in our state of bewilderment, because we know not where else to turn. Our nation is caught in the turmoil of war, our communities are facing racial unrest, and an increase in crime and delinquency accelerates yearly. Our young people and students seem to reject all outer authority, and exhibit little inner discipline. Even our own homes offer many of us little shelter from the disturbances of daily life, and our churches and synagogues seem torn with strife and dissension.

To whom, then, shall we turn, save to Thee Who has been our help in ages past, our hope for years to come, a shelter from stormy blasts and an eternal home? To Thee we turn with confidence and assurance that Thou art ever near to us, a very present help in trouble. May Thy presence be felt in our midst and may we take courage, rise up and live in the midst of these conflicts and fears in the strength that comes only from Thee through Thy Son Jesus Christ, in Whose Name we pray. Amen.

PRAYER FOR
SPIRITUAL STRENGTH

HEAVENLY FATHER, the Father of all wisdom, understanding and true strength, I beseech Thee, look mercifully upon me, and send Thy Holy Spirit into my breast; that when I must join to fight in the field for the glory of Thy holy Name, then I, being strengthened with the defence of Thy right hand, may manfully stand in the confession of Thy faith, and of Thy truth, and continue in the same unto the end of my life, through our Lord, Jesus Christ. Amen.

PRAYER FOR PEACE

GOD, from Whom all holy desires, all good counsels, and all just works do proceed; give unto Thy servants that peace which the world cannot give; that our hearts may be set to obey Thy commandments, and also that by Thee, we, being defended from the fear of our enemies, may pass our time in rest and quietness; through the merits of Jesus Christ our Savior. Amen.

PRAYER FOR
SUBMISSION TO GOD'S WILL

St. Teresa, *who wrote this prayer, is the only woman ever given the title of Doctor of the Church. She founded the order of Discalced Carmelites in her native Spain in the 16th century and became one of the great mystics of Christianity. It would be false, however, to see her only in the cloister, lost to the world in her prayers. Of prayer she wrote: "the best prayer, and most pleasing to God, is that which brings on improvement, showing itself in good works."*

Govern all by Thy wisdom, O Lord, so that my soul may always be serving Thee as Thou dost will, and not as I may choose. Do not punish me, I beseech Thee, by granting that which I wish or ask, if it offend Thy love, which would always live in me. Let me die to myself, so I may serve Thee: let me live to Thee, Who in Thyself art the true life. Amen.

A DAILY PRAYER

O God, our heavenly Father, renew in us the sense of Thy gracious presence, and let it be a constant impulse within us to peace, trustfulness, and courage on our pilgrimage. Let us hold Thee fast with a loving and adoring heart, and let our affections be fixed on Thee, so that the unbroken communion of our

[73]

hearts with Thee may accompany us whatsoever we do, through life and in death. Teach us to pray heartily; to listen for Thy voice within, and never to stifle its warnings. Behold, we bring our poor hearts as a sacrifice unto Thee: come and fill Thy sanctuary, and suffer naught impure to enter there. O Thou Who art love, let Thy divine spirit flow like a river through our whole souls, and lead us in the right way till we pass by a peaceful death into the land of promise. Amen.

PSALM 47

CLAP YOUR HANDS, all ye people; shout unto God with the voice of triumph.

For the Lord most high is terrible; He is a great King over all the earth.

He shall subdue the people under us, and the nations under our feet.

He shall choose our inheritance for us, the excellency of Jacob whom He loved. Selah.

God is gone up with a shout, the Lord with the sound of a trumpet.

Sing praises to God, sing praises: sing praises unto our King, sing praises.

For God is the King of all the earth: sing ye praises with understanding.

God reigneth over the heathen: God sitteth upon the throne of His holiness.

The princes of the people are gathered together, even the people of the God of Abraham: for the shields of the earth belong unto God: He is greatly exalted.

PRAYER FOR
OUR COUNTRY

LMIGHTY GOD, Who hast given us this good land for our heritage; we humbly beseech Thee that we may always prove ourselves a people mindful of Thy favor and glad to do Thy will. Bless our land with honorable industry, sound learning, and pure manners. Save us from violence, discord, and confusion; from pride and arrogancy, and from every evil way. Defend our liberties, and fashion into one united people the multitudes brought hither out of many kindreds and tongues. Endue with the spirit of wisdom those to whom in Thy Name we entrust the authority of government, that there may be justice and peace at home, and that, through obedience to Thy law, we may show forth Thy praise among the nations of the earth. In the time of prosperity, fill our hearts with thankfulness, and in the day of trouble, suffer not our trust in Thee to fail; all which we ask through Jesus Christ our Lord. Amen.

GEORGE WASHINGTON'S
PRAYER

LMIGHTY GOD, we make our earnest prayer that Thou wilt keep the United States in Thy holy protection; that Thou wilt incline the hearts of the citizens to cultivate a spirit of subordination and obedience to government and entertain a brotherly affection and love for one another and for their fellow-citizens of the United States at large. And, finally, that Thou wilt most graciously be pleased to dispose us all to do justice, to love mercy, and to demean ourselves with that charity, humility, and pacific temper of mind which were the characteristics of the Divine Author of our blessed religion and, without which we can never hope to be a happy nation. Grant our supplication, we beseech Thee, through Jesus Christ our Lord. Amen.

THE EISENHOWER PRAYER

This brief prayer was written personally by GENERAL DWIGHT D. EISENHOWER *as the beginning of his first inaugural address, on January 20, 1953. The general said that he was inspired to write the prayer as he returned to his hotel room from church, shortly before he was to take his oath as president. He said he had only "three to five minutes" in which to write it and have his secretary add it to the text of his address. Eisenhower said he thought of the prayer as "one simple way to show that I did have the conviction and the faith that there exists a Supreme Being Who has the final authority over our lives and the events on this earth." He added: "I wanted that little prayer to express my conviction that we should try to live according to the precepts of all the basic religions."*

ALMIGHTY GOD, as we stand here at this moment my future associates in the executive branch of government join me in beseeching that Thou will make full and complete our dedication to the service of the people in this throng, and their fellow citizens everywhere. Give us, we pray, the power to discern clearly right from wrong, and allow all our words and actions to be governed thereby, and by the laws of this land. Especially we pray that our concern shall be for all the people regardless of station, race, or calling. May cooperation be permitted and be the mutual aim of those who, under the concepts of our Constitution, hold to differing political faiths, so that all may work for the good of our beloved country and Thy glory. Amen.

PRAYER FOR
THE PRESIDENT AND ALL IN
CIVIL AUTHORITY

LORD, our Governor, Whose glory is in all the world; we commend this nation to Thy merciful care, that being guided by Thy providence, we may dwell secure in Thy peace. Grant to The President of the United States, and to all in authority, wisdom and strength to know and to do Thy will. Fill them with the love of truth and righteousness; and make them ever mindful of their calling to serve this people in Thy fear; through Jesus Christ our Lord, Who liveth and reigneth with Thee and the Holy Ghost, one God, world without end. Amen.

PRAYER FOR THE ARMY

LORD GOD OF HOSTS, stretch forth, we pray Thee, Thine almighty arm to strengthen and protect the soldiers of our country. Support them in the day of battle, and in the time of peace keep them safe from all evil; endue them with courage and loyalty; and grant that in all things they may serve without reproach; through Jesus Christ our Lord. Amen.

PRAYER FOR THE NAVY

ETERNAL LORD GOD, Who alone spreadest out the heavens, and rulest the raging of the sea; vouchsafe to take into Thy almighty and most gracious protection our country's Navy, and all who serve therein. Preserve them from the dangers of the sea, and from the violence of the enemy; that they may be a safeguard unto the United States of America, and a security for such as pass on the seas upon their lawful occasions; that the inhabitants of our land may in peace and quietness serve Thee, our God, to the glory of Thy Name; through Jesus Christ our Lord. Amen.

PRAYER FOR THE AIR FORCE

O LORD, King of all the universe, God of the heavens and the earth, Thou Who supported David in his hour of battle, extend Thy sustaining hand to the men of our Air Force; lift them up that they may be the shield of Thy people, so that all this nation in Thy peace may sing your glories, for evermore. Amen.

A PRAYER FOR THE ASTRONAUTS

His Eminence, Terence Cardinal Cooke, Archbishop of New York, is the author of this prayer which fills a need unique to our own day and displays the reach of faith through the ages from psalmist to scientist, and through the universe from man to Moon.

Heavenly Father, Whose Almighty Hand fashioned the universe and Whose presence pervades the farthest star, be with us today as we open wide our minds and hearts to think prayerfully of our gallant heroes. Grant, O Lord, that as we honor them, we may also be inspired by their great qualities of mind and spirit—their daring courage, their unselfishness, their strong faith in You. Above all, let us ever be grateful to You for their safety in their journey through space and their return to the good earth.

Grant, O Heavenly Father, that in our search into the mysteries of Your universe, we may always keep the deep reverence these men have shown. Help us to recognize, as they do, Your creative and sustaining hand everywhere and in all things. Cause us to marvel, as they do, at the glories of Your creation and let this wonderment deepen our wisdom.

Bless, O Father, these men who have done so much for our country and our world. Bless and reward their families and loved ones, who have truly shared their prayer and their work. Bless abundantly the many dedicated people whose talent and devoted efforts make these journeys possible. Bless our country and make the exploration of space a great step toward peace and happiness for all mankind. Amen.

E PRAISE Thee, O God; we acknowledge
Thee to be the Lord.
All the earth doth worship Thee, the Father everlasting.
To Thee all angels cry aloud, the heavens, and all the powers
 therein;
To Thee cherubim and seraphim continually do cry,
Holy, Holy, Holy, Lord God of Savaoth;
Heaven and earth are full of the majesty of Thy glory.
The glorious company of the Apostles praise Thee.
The goodly fellowship of the Prophets praise Thee.
The noble army of martyrs praise Thee.
The holy church throughout all the world doth acknowledge
 Thee;
The Father, of an infinite majesty;
Thine adorable, true, and only Son;
Also the Holy Ghost, the Comforter.

Thou art the King of Glory, O Christ,
Thou art the everlasting Son of the Father.
When Thou tookest upon Thee to deliver man, Thou didst
 humble Thyself to be born of a virgin.
When Thou hadst overcome the sharpness of death, Thou didst
 open the kingdom of heaven to all believers.
Thou sittest at the right hand of God, in the glory of the Father.
We believe that Thou shalt come to be our judge.
We therefore pray Thee, help Thy servants, Whom Thou hast
 redeemed with Thy precious blood.
Make them to be numbered with Thy saints, in glory everlasting.

O Lord, save Thy people, and bless Thine heritage.
Govern them, and lift them up for ever.
Day by day we magnify Thee;

And we worship Thy Name ever, world without end. Vouchsafe,
O Lord, to keep us this day without sin.
O Lord, have mercy upon us, have mercy upon us.
O Lord, let Thy mercy be upon us, as our trust is in Thee.
O Lord, in Thee have I trusted; let me never be confounded.

THANKSGIVING
FOR DELIVERANCE
FROM NATIONAL PERIL

ALMIGHTY GOD, Who art a strong tower of defence unto
Thy servants against the face of their enemies; we yield Thee
praise and thanksgiving for our deliverance from those great and
apparent dangers wherewith we were compassed. We acknowledge it Thy goodness that we were not delivered over as a prey
unto them; beseeching Thee still to continue such Thy mercies
towards us, that all the world may know that Thou art our
Savior and mighty Deliverer; through Jesus Christ our Lord.
Amen.

PRAYER FOR LOVE OF GOD

ALMIGHTY GOD, unto Whom all hearts are open, all
desires known, and from Whom no secrets are hid; cleanse the
thoughts of our hearts by the inspiration of Thy Holy Spirit,
that we may perfectly love Thee, and worthily magnify Thy
holy Name; through Christ our Lord. Amen.

PRAYER FOR THOSE
WITH WHOM
WE HAVE A QUARREL

I OFFER UP unto Thee my prayers and intercessions, for those especially who have in any manner hurt, grieved, or found fault with me, or who have done me any damage or displeasure.

For all those also whom, at any time, I may have vexed, troubled, burdened, and scandalized, by words or deeds, knowingly or in ignorance; that Thou wouldst grant us all equally pardon for our sins, and for our offenses against each other.

Take away from our hearts, O Lord, all suspiciousness, indignation, wrath and contention, and whatsoever may hurt charity and lessen brotherly love.

Have mercy, O Lord, have mercy on those that crave Thy mercy, give grace unto them that stand in need thereof, and make us such as that we may be worthy to enjoy Thy grace, and go forward to life eternal. Amen.

PRAYER FOR CHARITY

O GOD, the enlightener of men, Who of all graces givest the most abundant blessing upon heavenly love; we beseech Thee to cleanse us from selfishness, and grant us, for Thy love, so to love our brethren that we may be Thy children upon earth; and thereby, walking in Thy truth, attain to Thy unspeakable joy, Who art the giver of life to all who truly love Thee. Grant this prayer, O Lord. Amen.

MEEK AND LOWLY

In what is probably his best known sentence, the Apostle Paul wrote, in his first Epistle to the Corinthians (xiii 13), "And now abideth faith, hope, charity, these three; but the greatest of these is charity." It remained for an obscure poet, CHARLES JEFFREYS, to remind us that Paul, when he wrote "great" did not mean formidable, or beyond the reach of us who lack greatness. A prolific 19th century English composer, Stephen Glover, provided the music which helped preserve this little poem of Jeffreys' as a hymn.

MEEK AND lowly, pure and holy,
  Chief among the "Blessed Three,"
Turning sadness into gladness,
  Heav'n-born art thou, Charity!
Pity dwelleth in thy bosom,
  Kindness reigneth o'er thy heart;
Gentle thoughts alone can sway thee,
  Judgment hath in thee no part.

Meek and lowly, pure and holy,
  Chief among the "Blessed Three,"
Turning sadness into gladness,
  Heav'n-born art thou, Charity.

Hoping ever, failing never,
  Tho' deceived, believing still;
Long abiding, all confiding,
  To thy heav'nly Father's will;

Never weary of well-doing,
  Never fearful of the end;
Claiming all mankind as brothers,
  Thou dost all alike befriend.

Meek and lowly, pure and holy,
  Chief among the "Blessed Three,"
Turning sadness into gladness,
  Heav'n-born art thou, Charity.

PRAYER FOR
THE SUCCESS OF
A CHARITABLE WORK

GOD, the Father of the forsaken, the help of the weak, the supplier of the needy, Who has diffused and proportioned Thy gifts to body and soul, in such sort that all may acknowledge and perform the joyous duty of mutual service; Who teachest us that love towards the race of man is the bond of perfection, and the imitation of Thy blessed self; open our eyes and touch our hearts, that we may see and do, both for this world and for that which is to come, the things which belong unto our peace. Strengthen me in the work I have undertaken; give me counsel and wisdom, perseverance, faith and zeal, and in Thine own good time, and according to Thy pleasure, prosper the issue. Pour into me a spirit of humility; let nothing be done but in devout obedience to Thy will, thankfulness for Thine unspeakable mercies, and love to Thine adorable Son Jesus Christ. Amen.

[84]

PRAYER FOR PERSEVERANCE

This prayer is from the REVEREND DOCTOR JUDAH NADICH, *Rabbi of the Park Avenue Synagogue, in Manhattan.*

E PRAY with the Psalmist:
"To declare Thy loving kindness in the morning and Thy faithfulness in the night seasons"—
Help us, O Lord to fulfill this prayer in our own lives.

May we in the morning of promise and fulfillment recognize that Thou, in Thy ever-present kindness, hath given us life and the many bounties we enjoy. Keep us humble and thankful in success and let not abundance and strength dull our hearts or make us forgetful of the lives and sensitivities of others.

In adversity may we remain strong in faith in Thy unfailing benevolence and in the justice of Thy acts, though our frail minds may not comprehend the workings of Thy will.

Let neither pride nor despair bar us from recognizing Thy hand in all that comes over us and enable us thus to attain peace in the midst of the fretfulness and fury of our personal lives, the tumultuous life of our nation and the troubled life of humanity of which we are a part. Amen.

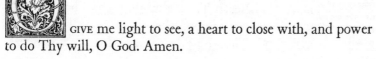GIVE me light to see, a heart to close with, and power to do Thy will, O God. Amen.

PSALM FOR THE TROUBLED

This is the Third Psalm

LORD, how are they increased that trouble me! many are they that rise up against me.

Many there be which say of my soul, There is no help for him in God. Selah.

But Thou, O Lord, art a shield for me; my glory, and the lifter up of mine head.

I cried unto the Lord with my voice, and He heard me out of His holy hill. Selah.

I laid me down and slept; I awaked; for the Lord sustained me.

I will not be afraid of ten thousands of people, that have set themselves against me round about.

Arise, O Lord; save me, O my God: for Thou hast smitten all mine enemies upon the cheek bone; Thou hast broken the teeth of the ungodly.

Salvation belongeth unto the Lord: Thy blessing is upon Thy people. Selah.

PRAYER IN
TIME OF TROUBLE

GRANT WE beseech Thee, almighty God, that we, who in our tribulation are yet of good cheer because of Thy loving-kindness, may find Thee mighty to save from all dangers, through Jesus Christ. Amen.

PRAYER IN TIME OF
SPIRITUAL DIFFICULTY

JOHN WOOLMAN, *author of this prayer, was an early 18th century member of the Society of Friends—a Quaker. He was one of the earliest and most effective foes of slavery, pioneering with sweet gentleness the course which other celebrated American churchmen were to follow fifty to 100 years later. His mission took him from his native New Jersey to one Meeting after another across Colonial America. Although Friends do not properly have established prayers, Woolman in his* Journal *and in other writings committed to paper many of the prayerful thoughts which were part of his daily life and won for him from one commentator the title of "uncanonized saint." This selection might well be called "a prayer that was answered."*

LORD MY GOD! the amazing horrors of darkness were gathered round me, and covered me all over, and I saw no way to go forth; I felt the depth and extent of the misery of my fellow creatures separated from the Divine harmony, and it was heavier than I could bear, and I was crushed down under it; I lifted up my hand, I stretched out my arm, but there was none to help me; I looked round about, and was amazed. In the depths of misery, O Lord, I remembered that Thou art omnipotent; and that I had called Thee Father; and I felt that I loved Thee, and I was made quiet in my will, and I waited for deliverance from Thee. Thou hadst pity upon me, when no man could help me; I saw that meekness under suffering was showed to us in the most affecting example of Thy Son, and Thou taughtest me to follow Him, and I said, "Thy will, O Father, be done!"

THANKSGIVING FOR CONVERSION

This is by St. Augustine, *fifth century Bishop of Hippo, one of the great theologians of Christianity. It is adapted from his autobiography,* Confessions—*a book-length prayer of praise to God for the gift of faith Augustine obtained comparatively late in life.*

LATE HAVE I loved Thee, O Thou eternal truth and goodness: late have I sought Thee, my Father! But Thou didst seek me, and when Thou shined forth upon me, then I knew Thee and learned to love Thee. I thank Thee, O my light, that Thou didst thus shine upon me; that Thou didst teach my soul what Thou wouldst be to me, and didst incline Thy face in pity upon me. Thou, Lord, hast become my hope, my comfort, my strength, my all! In Thee doth my soul rejoice. The darkness vanished from before mine eyes, and I beheld Thee, the Sun of Righteousness. When I loved darkness, I knew Thee not, but wandered from night to night. But Thou didst lead me out of that blindness; Thou didst take me by the hand, call me to Thee, and now I can thank Thee, and Thy mighty voice which hath penetrated to my inmost heart. Amen.

GLORIA PATRI

GLORY BE to the Father, and to the Son, and to the Holy Ghost;

As it was in the beginning, is now, and ever shall be, world without end. Amen.

A PRIVATE PRAYER AT
THE BEGINNING OF DAY

This prayer was submitted to Treasured Volume *by the* REVEREND DOCTOR BEN M. HERBSTER, *who is President of the United Church of Christ.*

HE NIGHT has gone, the day has dawned. Life has given me a new chance. I really do not deserve another opportunity. Too often I have played fast and loose with the moments which I have had. I have used them selfishly, carelessly, prodigally. Father forgive, forgive my foolishness.

Teach me the worth of time and the tragedy of wasted opportunity. Set me on a new course that shall cause me to employ my life in ways that are constructive. Time is so priceless. We shall not pass this way again!

I pray for people all over the world who must bear more than their fair share of the burdens of this life. Use me to relieve them of the injustice which we put upon their shoulders. Set me to work this day to establish justice and peace on earth.

We pray for those whom I call "family." My life is so rich because of them and how often I have not been grateful, nor have I returned love for love. Help me to see I would be so much less than I am without them. Teach me once again that I am a part of all whom I meet.

Help me make this a "good day" for all upon whom the shadow of my life shall fall.

Keep me until the night lowers and another day dawns, and I have another chance to make use of the opportunities that You have given me.

In Christ's Name we pray. Amen.

[89]

PRAYER OF THE SICK

GOD, I am sorely stricken; but in my pain let me not forget Thee. Thou art long-suffering and patient; and in Thy great mercy Thou wilt forgive the murmuring lips and the weary soul. Give me understanding to know that this bitter trial has come upon me for my welfare, that I may not despise Thy chastening.

In all humility I lay bare my soul before Thee and ask Thy pardon for my shortcomings. A broken and contrite heart Thou wilt not despise.

May it be Thy will to aid those who would bring me to a speedy recovery. I thank Thee for all the dear ones whose sympathy and care have eased my suffering. Mayest Thou answer the prayers of our hearts. Heal me, that I may again praise Thy Name in the congregation of Israel. Amen.

PRAYER SAID BY THE SICK ON RECOVERY

MY GOD, Father of mercy. I thank Thee for the healing which Thy loving-kindness has wrought for me. Thou hast raised me from a bed of sickness. When I was racked with pain, when my strength was spent and my very soul within me trembled, Thou didst not forsake me. Thou hast saved me, keeping me in the land of the living, restoring me to health and the sweet companionship of my beloved ones.

With great rejoicing therefore, and with all my soul, I bring to Thee the offering of my thanksgiving. Help me so to use my renewed strength that I may be of service to Thee by being a blessing to my fellow men. Amen.

PENITENT'S PRAYER

This all-encompassing plea for forgiveness for offenses against God comes from a 16th century book of private devotions.

FORGIVE ME my sins, O Lord, forgive me the sins of my youth and the sins of mine age, the sins of my soul and the sins of my body, my secret and my whispering sins, my presumptuous and my crying sins, the sins that I have done to please myself and the sins that I have done to please others. Forgive me those sins which I know, and those sins which I know not; forgive them, O Lord, forgive them all of Thy great goodness. Amen.

O MERCIFUL GOD

O MOST MERCIFUL and gracious God, Thou fountain of all mercy and blessing, Thou hast opened the hand of Thy mercy to fill me with blessings, and the sweet effects of Thy loving kindness. Thou feedest us like a shepherd, Thou lovest us as a friend, and thinkest on us perpetually, as a careful mother on her helpless babe, and art exceeding merciful to all that fear Thee. As Thou hast spread Thy hand upon me for a covering, so also enlarge my heart with thankfulness; and let Thy gracious favors and loving kindness endure for ever and ever upon Thy servant; and grant that what Thou hast sown in mercy, may spring up in duty; and let Thy grace so strengthen my purposes that I may sin no more, but walk in the paths of Thy commandments; that I, living here to the glory of Thy Name, may at last enter into the glory of my Lord, to spend a whole eternity in giving praise to Thy ever glorious Name. Amen.

PRAYER FOR
A CLEAN TONGUE

O MY GOD! guard my tongue from evil and my lips from speaking guile; and to such as curse me let my soul be dumb, yea, let my soul be unto all as the dust. Open my heart to Thy law, and let my soul pursue Thy commandments. If any design against me, speedily make their counsel of no effect, and frustrate their designs. Do it for the sake of Thy name, do it for the sake of Thy power, do it for the sake of Thy holiness, do it for the sake of Thy law. In order that Thy beloved ones may be delivered, O save by Thy power, and answer me. Let the words of my mouth and the meditation of my heart be acceptable before Thee, O Lord, my rock and my redeemer. He Who maketh peace in His high places, may He make peace for us and for all Israel, and say ye, Amen.

PRAYER OF RESOLUTION

MY GOD! I firmly resolve to fly from sin, and I implore Thee for Jesus' sake to grant me the grace of perseverance. And especially I am resolved that in every trial, taking refuge in Thy holy will, the prayer of my heart shall be, "O Lord! Thy will be done." Amen.

PRAYER FOR UNITY UNDER GOD

The REVEREND DOCTOR EUGENE C. BLAKE, *who submitted this prayer for* Treasured Volume, *is a native of St. Louis, Missouri, whose dedication to the Christian dream of one church has won international recognition: election to the key post of General Secretary of the General Secretariat of the World Council of Churches.*

GOD our heavenly Father we thank You that You have entrusted this world to us, Your children. Help us always to remember Your love for all mankind and teach us to strive for the unity of Your World. We praise You for its beauty and its wonders and for the privilege of living in a time when You have enabled man to extend his domain beyond the earthly planet.

We pray that You will continue to guide Your Church in all its endeavors to unity and thank You in all humility, for the visible signs expressed here today of our halting steps to heal the divisions of Your Church. We thank You for the pioneers of the ecumenical movement and pray that we will not lose their hope for the visible unity of Your Church renewed for mission and service. We are especially grateful for visions of a wider ecumenism which sees all Your people, within and outside the Church, as one family of mankind, and for our interdependent life and our common hopes and aspirations.

We ask, heavenly Father, for Your forgiveness that we have so often failed to recognise the injustice and cruelty of man to man which we, Your servants support by inaction. We ask Your forgiveness for our acceptance of the inadequacies of the social order, nationally and internationally, and pray that You will give us courage to be bold in seeking justice for all Your children. Help

[93]

us, O God, not to be frightened of the change and challenge of our time but to see that You are always among us, not only to comfort and console, but also to give us visions of the new world which You are making in our midst.

You have taught us, Father, through Jesus Christ, that You love Your children equally. Help us in our lives with our brothers to affirm Your love, praying that in Your power You will use us as instruments of Your blessing upon:

> The hungry, the homeless and the poor;
> The casualties of our industrialised societies;
> Political prisoners and the oppressed;
> Those who are discriminated against because of
>   color or nationality;
> Those who find no reason to believe in You.

Grant, O Father, Your blessing to all those who have authority over the people of this nation and the many nations of the world, that they may exercise this authority with wisdom, humility and compassion.

All these things we pray in the name of our Lord, Jesus Christ. Amen.

PRAYER FOR THE LONELY

BE THOU present with me, O Lord, in every time and place. Let this be my consolation, to be cheerfully willing to do without all human comfort. And, if Thy consolation be wanting, let Thy will and just trial of me be unto me as the greatest comfort. Amen.

TRAVELER'S PRAYER

LORD of the universe, the whole world is full of Thy glory. Wherever I may journey, Thou art near me to shield and to guide. "If I take the wings of the morning and dwell in the uttermost part of the sea; even there would Thy hand lead me, and Thy right hand would hold me."

With grateful heart I thank Thee, O Lord, for all Thy guidance in the past. Thou hast been a light to my path. Thou hast shielded me on my journeying in the past and brought me safely back to my home. Now that I begin a new journey, I turn to Thee, O Lord, confident of Thy guidance. O guard Thou me against the perils of the road. Keep me in health and bring me safely to my destination. Grant that this journey be not in vain but that the purposes of my travel be fulfilled. Shield me on my return and bring me back in health to my dear ones. Bestow Thy blessing upon me as I depart and when, with Thy help, I shall return. Amen.

PRAYER FOR
TRAVEL BY AUTOMOBILE

O GOD, Who drew Thy prophet Elias to heaven in a fiery chariot, Who saw Mary and Joseph and their Child safe into the land of Egypt, Whose loving-kindness has brought us this far on the road of life, be with us on the highways and by-ways of this world that we may enjoy the works of Thy creation in peace and safety and sing Your praises now as we hope to do forevermore. Amen.

[95]

PRAYER FOR
TRAVEL BY PLANE

GOD, Whose glory is reflected from the wings of angelic choirs, Whose host of ministering angels would bear up Thy Son lest His foot be dashed against a rock, hear this prayer: that your faithful servant embarking now on a journey may enjoy Thy safe protection, be guarded from all danger, and return, to the glory of Thy Name. Amen.

PRAYER FOR
PERSON GOING TO SEA

ETERNAL GOD, Who alone spreadest out the heavens, and rulest the raging of the sea; we commit to Thy almighty protection, Thy servant, for whose preservation on the great deep our prayers are desired. Guard him/her, we beseech Thee, from the dangers of the sea, from sickness, from the violence of enemies, and from every evil to which he/she may be exposed. Conduct him/her in safety to the haven where he/she would be, with a grateful sense of Thy mercies; through Jesus Christ our Lord. Amen.

THANKSGIVING
FOR FAIR WEATHER

LORD GOD, Who hast justly humbled us by Thy late visitation of us with immoderate rain and waters, and in Thy mercy has relieved and comforted our souls by this seasonable and blessed change of weather; we praise and glorify Thy holy Name for this Thy mercy, and will always declare Thy loving-kindness from generation to generation; through Jesus Christ our Lord. Amen.

THANKSGIVING FOR A SAFE RETURN FROM A JOURNEY

OST GRACIOUS Lord, Whose mercy is over all Thy works; we praise Thy holy Name that Thou hast been pleased to conduct in safety, through the perils of his/her way, this Thy servant, who now desireth to return his/her thanks unto Thee in Thy holy Church. May he/she be duly sensible of Thy merciful providence towards him/her, and ever express his/her thankfulness by a holy trust in Thee, and obedience to Thy laws, through Jesus Christ our Lord. Amen.

MORNING PRAYER

E GIVE THEE thanks, holy Lord, Father Almighty, ever-lasting God, Who hast been pleased to bring us through the night to the hours of morning; we pray Thee to grant us to pass this day without sin, so that at eventide we may again give thanks to Thee, through Jesus Christ our Lord. Amen.

PRAYER IN PENANCE

God, Whose nature and property is ever to have mercy and to forgive; receive our humble petitions; and though we be tied and bound with the chain of our sins, yet let the pitifulness of Thy great mercy loose us; for the honor of Jesus Christ, our mediator and advocate. Amen.

The Lord bless us, and keep us. The Lord make His face to shine upon us, and be gracious unto us. The Lord lift up His countenance upon us, and give us peace, both now and evermore. Amen.

MY DESIRE

Lord, this is all my desire—to walk along the path of life that Thou hast appointed me, even as Jesus my Lord would walk along it, in steadfastness of faith, in meekness of spirit, in lowliness of heart, in gentleness of love. And because outward events have so much power in scattering my thoughts and disturbing the inward peace in which alone the voice of Thy spirit is heard, do Thou gracious Lord, calm and settle my soul by that subduing power which alone can bring all thoughts and desires of the heart into captivity to Thyself. All I have is Thine; do Thou with all as seems best to Thy divine will; for I know not what is best. Let not the cares or duties of this life press on me too heavily; but lighten my burden, that I may follow Thy way in quietness, filled with thankfulness for Thy mercy, and rendering acceptable service unto Thee. Amen.

[98]

A PRAYER FOR A SHARE
IN THE GLORY OF HEAVEN

The RIGHT REVEREND C. KILMER MYERS, *Bishop of California,*
suggested this prayer for inclusion in this Treasured Volume.
He says it is one of his personal favorites. It is from the Book of
Common Prayer, *for the Feast of the Transfiguration of Christ*
—August 6.

GOD, Who on the mount didst reveal to chosen wit-
nesses Thine only-begotten Son wonderfully transfigured, in
raiment white and glistening; mercifully grant that we, being
delivered from the disquietude of this world, may be permitted
to behold the King in His beauty, Who with Thee, O Father, and
Thee, O Holy Ghost, liveth and reigneth, one God, world without end. Amen.

PRAYER FOR GRACE

LORD, our heavenly Father, almighty and everlasting
God, Who hast safely brought us to the beginning of this day;
defend us in the same with Thy mighty power; and grant that
this day we fall into no sin, neither run into any kind of danger;
but that all our doings, being ordered by Thy governance, may
be righteous in Thy sight; through Jesus Christ our Lord. Amen.

PRAYER FOR
UNION WITH GOD

I WOULD, dear Jesus, I could break
The hedge that creeds and hearsay make,
And, like the first disciples, be
In person led and taught by Thee.

I read Thy words, so strong and sweet;
I seek the footprints of Thy feet;
But men so mystify the trace,
I long to see Thee face to face.

Wouldst Thou not let me at Thy side,
In Thee, in Thee so sure confide?
Like John, upon Thy breast recline,
And feel Thy heart make mine divine?

PRAYER FOR
THE AFFLICTED

ALMIGHTY and everlasting God, the comfort of the sad,
the strength of sufferers, let the prayers of those that cry out of
any tribulation come unto Thee; that all may rejoice to find
that Thy mercy is present with them in their afflictions; through
Jesus Christ our Lord. Amen.

PARENTS' PRAYER ON
THE BIRTH OF A SON

O LORD, source of all life, we lift our hearts in thanks unto Thee for the life of the son whom Thou hast granted unto us and who has been entrusted by Thee to our care.

Bestow Thy blessing upon our little one. May he grow in strength of body, mind and spirit. May he develop in the love of Thee and of his fellowmen to the end that his life may glorify Thy Name, be a blessing unto society, and a joy unto himself.

May the merits of the fathers and mothers in Israel rest upon him and guide him in paths pleasing in Thy sight.

Give unto us, O Father, the wisdom, courage, and faith that we as parents may perform our sacred duties in accordance with Thy will. Amen.

PARENTS' PRAYER ON
THE BIRTH OF
A DAUGHTER

OUR HEAVENLY FATHER, Thou hast been exceedingly gracious unto us. From Thee unto us has come the life of our daughter. Our hearts are filled with gratitude. We would express our thanks not only with words but with our striving to do Thy will towards her whom Thou hast created in Thine image.

Be Thou her guide on life's path. Keep her life from all evil. Direct her spirit to the good, true and beautiful. May her life fulfill the ideal:

"Grace is deceitful and beauty is vain, but a woman that feareth the Lord shall be praised."

Consecrate us, O God, to the responsibilities of parenthood and make us worthy of Thy love and mercy. Amen.

THANKSGIVING OF WOMEN AFTER CHILDBIRTH

ALMIGHTY GOD, we give Thee humble thanks for that Thou hast been graciously pleased to preserve, through the great pain and peril of childbirth, this woman—Thy servant—who desireth now to offer her praises and thanksgivings unto Thee. Grant, we beseech Thee, most merciful Father, that she, through Thy help, may faithfully live according to Thy will in this life, and also may be partaker of everlasting glory in the life to come; through Jesus Christ our Lord. Amen.

A PARENT'S PRAYER

LORD, make me a kind and tender parent, truly careful and solicitous to promote the welfare and happiness of my children. Let Thy good spirit assist me to form in their tender minds the principles of virtue and religion, to teach them to remember Thee, their Creator, in the days of their youth, and to bring them up in Thy fear and love: let me make it my constant care and endeavor to wean them from all pride and vanity, and to set before them the example of a holy and religious life.

O let the powerful efficacy of Thy good Spirit root out of their hearts all corrupt and sinful affections; and, instead, sow the incorruptible seed of Thy grace, that they may become partakers of Thy divine nature, and may bring forth in their lives the fruits of righteousness and true holiness.

Defend them, O Lord, I beseech Thee, against the evils and temptations of this world, and grant that they may never be led away by the wicked customs and examples, the lusts and vanities of it; but obediently keeping Thy holy will and commandments, and walking in the same all the days of their lives, may be instruments of Thy glory, by doing good in their generation; and after they have served Thee faithfully in this world, may hereafter be made partakers of everlasting happiness in that which is to come, through Jesus Christ our Lord. Amen.

CRADLE HYMN

The Reverend Isaac Watts *won recognition as a poet among his early 19th century English colleagues for work which few of them attempted: the composition of hymns. Some 600 came from his pen. Many are still sung today, including this prayerful lullaby.*

Hush, my babe, lie still and slumber,
    Holy angels guard thy bed.
Heav'nly blessings without number,
    Gently falling on thy head.

How much better thou'rt attended,
Than the Son of God could be;
When from heaven He descended,
And became a child like thee.

Soft and easy is thy cradle,
Coarse and hard thy Savior lay:
When His birthplace was a stable
And His softest bed was hay.
May'st thou learn to know and fear Him,
Love and serve Him all thy days;
Then to dwell forever near Him,
Tell His love and sing His praise.

PRAYER ON NAMING A CHILD

PRAISE AND gratitude fill our hearts on this day as we bring to Thee, Almighty God, the dear child with which Thou hast blessed us. We dedicate it to a life of usefulness, honor and piety. We bestow upon it the name .... May that name be a token of every virtue. May Thy blessing attend our dear child, to guard it against every evil, and to keep it from every danger.

May it be worthy throughout life to be crowned with Thy benediction: May God bless thee and keep thee. May God let His countenance shine upon thee, and be gracious unto thee. May God lift up His countenance upon thee, and give thee peace. Amen.

A BENEDICTION

This blessing is three verses from Numbers (vi 24-26) in which Aaron, the first High Priest, tells his sons—all future priests—how a blessing may be given.

THE LORD bless thee, and keep thee:
The Lord make His face shine upon thee, and be gracious unto thee:
The Lord lift up His countenance upon thee, and give thee peace.
Amen.

MORNING PRAYER
FOR YOUNG CHILDREN

BLESSED art Thou, O Lord our God, King of the universe, Who removest sleep from mine eyes, and slumber from mine eyelids.
I give thanks unto Thee, O living and eternal King Who hast restored my soul unto me in mercy: great is Thy faithfulness.
Hear, O Israel: the Lord is our God, the Lord is One.
Blessed be His Name, Whose glorious kingdom is for ever and ever.
And thou shalt love the Lord thy God with all thine heart, and with all thy soul, and with all thy might. Amen.

NOW I LAY ME
DOWN TO SLEEP

Now I lay me down to sleep,
I pray Thee, Lord, my soul to keep.
If I should die before I wake
I pray Thee, Lord, my soul to take.
Amen.

PRAYER FOR CHILDREN

LORD JESUS CHRIST, Who dost embrace children with
the arms of Thy mercy, and dost make them living members of
Thy church; give them grace, we pray Thee, to stand fast in
Thy faith, to obey Thy word, and to abide in Thy love; that,
being made strong by Thy Holy Spirit, they may resist temptation and overcome evil, and may rejoice in the life that now is,
and dwell with Thee in the life that is to come; through Thy
merits, O merciful Savior, Who with the Father and the Holy
Ghost livest and reignest one God, world without end. Amen.

A BIRTHDAY PRAYER

ETERNAL GOD, Thou art the Master of our destiny and
the source of all life. Our times are in Thy hand. We thank Thee

day by day for Thy manifold blessings and, as year follows year, we are grateful that Thou has sustained us.

We gather today in special joy and thankfulness to share in the happiness of our dear . . . . It is Thou Who has granted him/her strength and life. Bless him/her, O Lord, with health and joy. Sustain him/her in times of sickness and console him/her in times of sorrow. Endow him/her with long life and abundance of blessing; and grant to us the joy of meeting, for many years, as on this day, a loving family in mutual reverence and unbroken unity.

Praised be Thou, O Lord our God, Who has kept us in life, sustained us and brought us to this happy day.

LORD, WHOSE
NAME IS LOVE

LORD, give us hearts never to forget Thy love; but to dwell therein whatever we do, whether we sleep or wake, live or die, or rise again to the life that is to come. For Thy love is eternal life and everlasting rest; for this is life eternal to know Thee and Thy infinite goodness. O let its flame never be quenched in our hearts; let it grow and brighten, till our whole souls are glowing and shining with its light and warmth. Be Thou our joy and hope, our strength and life, our shield and shepherd, our portion for ever. For happy are we if we continue in the love wherewith Thou hast loved us; holy are we when we love Thee steadfastly. Therefore, O Thou, Whose name and essence is love, enkindle our hearts, enlighten our understanding, sanctify our wills, and fill all the thoughts of our hearts, for Jesus Christ's sake. Amen.

A DAILY PRAYER

The REVEREND DOCTOR ROBERT J. MARSHALL, *who submitted this prayer, is president of the Lutheran Church in America.*

ETERNAL FATHER, at the beginning of a new day we pause to be conscious of Thy continual presence and care and to be strengthened by contemplating the energizing power of Thy Spirit for all the hours when other demands will require our concentration.

What is burdensome, help us to endure.

What is satisfying, help us to enjoy but not misuse.

In work, help us to meet the true needs of others.

In our associations, help us find the various specific meanings of love.

When a wrong besets us in ourselves or others, let us praise Thee for Thy forgiveness and let us search for the new way to right.

Let the purpose of our life be clear in our faithfulness to Jesus Christ our Lord. Amen.

O GOD, OUR STRENGTH

O GOD, for as much as our strength is in Thee, mercifully grant that Thy Holy Spirit may in all things direct and rule our hearts, through Jesus Christ our Lord. Amen.

PRAYER FOR PEACE

This prayer was submitted by the REVEREND DOCTOR OSWALD C. J. HOFFMANN *of whom it may be said that he has one of the broadest pastorates in the country—as Speaker on "The Lutheran Hour."*

GOD in Whose hands are the nations of the world, the powerful as well as the weak, by the might of Your Holy Spirit put down the pride, the anger, and the greed which cause one man to fight against another, one people to go to war against another.

Lead the nations of the world, O God, in the ways of peace, and let truth and justice everywhere prevail.

Save us from those national sins that expose us to Your judgment; from profaning Your most Holy Word, from injustice to the helpless and carelessness toward the poor, from the worldly spirit of doing and enjoying with no thought of You or of Your will.

Look upon us, Lord God, with forgiveness. We bring no recommendation for Your favor, O God, except that You have invited us, through Your Son, to come as we are, wearing our everyday clothes.

In the good and saving name of Jesus Christ, and by His kind invitation, we confess our sin, admit our guilt, ask Your forgiveness, and seek Your strength.

What will happen to us today or tomorrow, O God, we do not know. We do know nothing will happen that You have not forseen, desired, determined, directed. That is enough to know so that we may live in hope.

Make us honest, so that people can see integrity of heart on our faces and in our eyes. Give us faith to trust You, patience to bear what must be borne, love to warm the lives of others, and courage to go forward into tomorrow, having peace and joy in the knowledge of Your favor made known so marvelously to the whole world in the cross of Your Son, Jesus Christ. Amen.

PRAYER IN
TIME OF WAR

ALMIGHTY GOD, the supreme Governor of all things, Whose power no creature is able to resist, to Whom it belongeth justly to punish sinners, and to be merciful to those who truly repent; save and deliver us, we humbly beseech Thee, from the hands of our enemies; that we, being armed with Thy defence, may be preserved evermore from all perils, to glorify Thee, Who art the only giver of all victory; through the merits of Thy Son, Jesus Christ our Lord. Amen.

PRAYER FOR
ENLIGHTENMENT

GOD, with Whom is the well of life, and in Whose light we see light; increase in us, we beseech Thee, the brightness of Divine knowledge, whereby we may be able to reach Thy plenteous fountain; impart to our thirsting souls the draught of life, and restore to our darkened minds the light from heaven. Amen.

PRAYER IN EXALTATION OF GOD

This prayer, submitted to Treasured Volume *by the* REVEREND DOCTOR LOUIS FINKELSTEIN, *Chancellor of the Jewish Theological Seminary of America, is from the Jewish liturgy for the solemn occasions of New Year's Day—Rosh Hashanah, and Day of Atonement—Yom Kippur.*

Now, therefore, O Lord our God, impose Thine awe upon all Thy works, and Thy dread upon all that Thou hast created, that all works may revere Thee and all creatures prostrate themselves before Thee, that they may all form a single band to do Thy will with a perfect heart; even as we know, O Lord our God, that dominion is Thine, strength is in Thy hand, and might in Thy right hand, and that Thy Name is to be revered above all that Thou hast created.

PSALM 43

JUDGE ME, O God, and plead my cause against an ungodly nation: O deliver me from the deceitful and unjust man.

For Thou art the God of my strength: why dost Thou cast me off? why go I mourning because of the oppression of the enemy?

O send out Thy light and Thy truth: let them lead me; let them bring me unto Thy holy hill, and to Thy tabernacles.

Then will I go unto the altar of God, unto God my exceeding joy: yea, upon the harp will I praise Thee, O God my God.

Why art Thou cast down O my soul? and why art thou disquieted within me? hope in God: for I shall yet praise Him, Who is the health of my countenance, and my God.

GOD OF THE UNIVERSES

The REVEREND DOCTOR EDWARD L. R. ELSON, *author of this prayer, is Minister of The National Presbyterian Church in Washington and Chaplain of the United States Senate.*

GOD of this universe and of the universes beyond, Who from the dawn of time, and through the processes of all history has been creating, from the formless void, the orbs and spheres in the unbounded immensity of space; and in Whose wisdom Thou hast placed man as Thy highest creation to have dominion over all Thy works; we thank Thee that it is given to us to live this day when earth-bound man, unfettered, soars lunar lands and spaces.

We thank Thee for man, for the majesty of his intellect, the depth of his soul, and for the sense of wonder and adventure with which Thou hast endowed him. As we hear again the words of Holy Writ, "What is man that Thou art mindful of him? . . . Thou crownest him with glory and honor, and didst set him over the works of Thy hands"; make us humble and thankful before Thy creation in man and in nature.

Be with us day by day in our labors. Teach us now and always that the true home of the soul is in Thee. Awaken us to the splendors of the new age that we may be pioneers in the vast reaches of the human spirit, and partners with Thee in the emancipation of man from hate and fear, from poverty and disease, from injustice and war, that a better world may come, and Thy will be done in and through us. In Thy holy Name, we pray. Amen.

PRAYER OF
THE DISTRESSED

ALMIGHTY GOD, the refuge of all that are distressed, grant unto us that, in all trouble of this our mortal life, we may flee to the knowledge of Thy loving kindness and tender mercy; that so, sheltering ourselves therein, the storms of life may pass over us, and not shake the peace of God that is within us. Whatsoever this life may bring us, grant that it may never take from us the full faith that Thou art our Father. Grant us Thy light, that we have life, through Jesus Christ our Lord. Amen.

PRAYER IN
TIME OF CALAMITY

O GOD, merciful and compassionate, Who art ever ready to hear the prayers of those who put their trust in Thee; graciously hearken to us who call upon Thee, and grant us Thy help in this our need; through Jesus Christ our Lord. Amen.

THANKSGIVING AFTER
PASSING THROUGH DANGER

M Y TIMES are in Thy hand, O God, and Thy tender mercies are ever near me.

Now that Thou hast delivered me, O God, from this unlooked for calamity, accept my most fervent words of prayer and thanks. According to my strength, help me to bring Thy comfort to all who suffer. Teach me to number my days, that I may apply my heart unto wisdom.

Help me to be calm in the presence of danger that I may bear all ordeals, trustful of Thy help.

Blessed art Thou, O Lord our God, King of the Universe, Who art the guardian of all Thy children, Who slumberest not and sleepest not. Amen.

SUMMER PRAYER

F ATHER, we thank Thee for this wondrous and lovely world in which Thou hast placed us. For the magnificent beauty of summer we thank Thee, for the storied promise of the spring which has gone by and Thine infinite love. We thank Thee that Thou waterest the earth with rain from Thine own sweet heavens, rejoicing the cattle on a thousand hills, which Thou also carest for, as for Thy chosen ones, and ministerest life to every little moss amid the stones of a city, and feedest the mighty forests which clothe with verdure our hills. We thank Thee that Thou givest us grass for the cattle, and corn to strengthen the frame of man, and orderest all things by number and measure

and weight, wielding the whole into a mighty mass of usefulness and a glorious orb of transcendent beauty. We bless Thee
for the beautiful amid the homely, the sublime among things
low, for the good amid evil things, and the eternal amid what
is transient, and daily passing from our eye.

We thank Thee for the happiness that attends us in our daily
life, for the joys of our daily work, for the success which Thou
givest to the labors of our hand, and the strength to our soul
which comes from our daily toil on the earth. We thank Thee
for the plain and common household joys of life, for the satis-
factions of friendship; for the blessedness of love in all the dear
relationships of mortal life. Father, we thank Thee for the large
sympathy with our brother-men everywhere, and that we know
that Thou has made them all alike in Thine own image, and
has destined all Thy children to toil on the earth, and to a glorious immortality of never-ending blessedness beyond the grave.

O Father, we pray Thee that we may never be false to the
great glories with which Thou surroundest us. So may Thy
kingdom come, and Thy will be done on earth as it is in heaven.
Amen.

GENERAL THANKSGIVING

ALMIGHTY GOD, Father of all mercies, we, Thine unworthy servants, do give Thee most humble and hearty thanks
for all Thy goodness and loving-kindness to us, and to all men;
(particularly to those who desire now to offer up their praises
and thanksgivings for Thy late mercies vouchsafed unto them).
We bless Thee for our creation, preservation, and all the blessings of this life; but above all, for Thine inestimable love in the
redemption of the world by our Lord Jesus Christ; for the

means of grace, and for the hope of glory. And, we beseech Thee, give us that due sense of all Thy mercies, that our hearts may be unfeignedly thankful; and that we show forth Thy praise, not only with our lips, but in our lives, by giving up our selves to Thy service, and by walking before Thee in holiness and righteousness all our days; through Jesus Christ, our Lord, to Whom, with Thee and the Holy Ghost, be all honor and glory, world without end. Amen.

PRAYER OF REPENTANCE

WE KNOW that we have sinned, and there is none to stand up in our behalf; let Thy great Name stand for our defence in time of trouble. We know that we have no good works of our own; deal with us in charity for Thy Name's sake. As a father hath mercy upon his children, so, O Lord, have mercy upon us, and save us for Thy Name's sake. Have pity upon Thy people; have mercy upon Thine inheritance; spare, we pray Thee, according to the abundance of Thy tender mercies; be gracious unto us and answer us, for charity is Thine, O Lord; Thou doest wondrous things at all times.

Look, we beseech Thee, and speedily have mercy upon Thy people for Thy Name's sake in Thine abundant mercies. O Lord our God, spare and be merciful; save the sheep of Thy pasture; let not wrath rule over us, for our eyes are bent upon Thee; save us for Thy Name's sake. Have mercy upon us for the sake of Thy covenant; look, and answer us in time of trouble, for salvation is Thine, O Lord. Our hope is in Thee, O God of forgiveness. We beseech Thee, forgive, O good and forgiving God, for Thou art a gracious and merciful God and King.

LIGHT OF OUR DARKNESS

This prayer is from BISHOP JAMES S. THOMAS, *Resident Bishop of the Iowa Area of the United Methodist Church.*

GOD, Who art the light of our darkness, we thank Thee for the many and varied ways in which Thou hast made Thyself known. Through the mystery of creation, we see the works of Thy hand. When the light of faith burns low, we consider ourselves and understand that we are marvelously made. Through the long history of man's experience with man, we see something of Thy will. The consequences of wrong remind us of what is right. The fruits of the spirit encourage us in what is true. Through the life and witness of prophets, martyrs, and saints, we are confirmed in our belief that Thou hast been present with men in all generations. And through Jesus Christ, our Lord, we see clearly the revelation of Thyself in human form.

Thou hast graciously called us to be servants. Grant us the vision to see the place where service is most helpful in a complex and troubled world. Give us the insight to see the tragedy of war for what it is. Help us to overcome the selfishness that often leads to our comfort while leaving the poverty of others unrelieved. Heal us of the hypocrisy of crying for peace while silently supporting the structures that lead to unrest.

In our best moments, we know we have been made for high purposes. Teach us what those purposes are and lead us toward them, we pray.

Where there is loneliness, help us to bring fellowship. In despair, help us to be apostles of hope. Use us according to Thy will for us and according to the needs of the world.

Through Jesus Christ, our Lord. Amen.

PRAYER FOR THE DISCOURAGED

This was selected from the prayers of the REVEREND DOCTOR W. A. CRISWELL, *pastor of the First Baptist Church, in Dallas, Texas, and President of the Southern Baptist Convention.*

UR LORD, if we are ever discouraged or defeated, forgive us. Oh, what victory, what glory, what celestial, heavenly, infinite prospect God hath reserved in store for those who love Him! Bless us as we go our way. Bring us back tomorrow, in the love and mercy and grace of Jesus, Amen.

PRAYER BEFORE
A CRUCIFIX

EHOLD, O kind and most sweet Jesus, I cast myself upon my knees in Thy sight, and with the most fervent desire of my soul I pray and beseech Thee that Thou wouldst impress upon my heart lively sentiments of faith, hope and charity, with a true contrition of my sins and a firm purpose of amendment; whilst with deep affection and grief of soul I ponder within myself and mentally contemplate Thy five wounds, having before my eyes the words which David the prophet put in Thy mouth regarding Thee: they have pierced My hands and feet, they have numbered all My bones.

THE APOSTLES' CREED

This is the simplest and oldest statement of Christian belief. One legend, published in the fifth century of the Christian era, attributed the formulation to the Twelve Apostles. According to the story the Apostles gathered together before spreading to the four corners of the earth and each cited one key doctrine of the faith he was carrying with him; thus the twelve doctrines of this creed. It was carried over into the churches of the Reformation with the specific approval of such preachers as Luther and Zwingli, and is still used in many churches although some prefer the phrase "Christian church" rather than "Catholic church" in the ninth article. This creed was advanced in 1927 as the basis of Christian unity at a World Conference of Faith and Order.

BELIEVE in God the Father Almighty, maker of heaven and earth: and in Jesus Christ His only Son our Lord: Who was conceived by the Holy Ghost, born of the Virgin Mary: suffered under Pontius Pilate, was crucified, dead, and buried: He descended into hell; the third day He rose again from the dead: He ascended into heaven, and sitteth on the right hand of God the Father Almighty: from thence He shall come to judge the quick and the dead.

I believe in the Holy Ghost: the holy Catholic Church: the communion of saints: the forgiveness of sins: the resurrection of the body: and the life everlasting. Amen.

ORD, take my lips, and speak through them; take my mind, and think through it; take my heart, and set it on fire.

There is no universal statement of Jewish belief, but probably the most widely accepted is the formulation of MAIMONIDES, *Spanish-born 12th century Jewish theologian and philosopher. In Maimonides' own time his creed was the center of a storm of controversy. Subsequent generations, however, have established it in the Jewish liturgy, not only in prose, but also in poetic form.*

THE LIVING GOD we praise, exalt, adore!
He was, He is, He will be evermore!

No unity like unto His can be:
Eternal, inconceivable is He.

No form, or shape has the incorporeal One,
Most holy He, past all comparison.

He was, ere aught was made in heaven, or earth,
But His existence has no date, or birth.

Lord of the Universe is He proclaimed,
Teaching His power to all His hand has framed.

He gave His gift of prophecy to those
In whom He gloried, whom He loved and chose.

No prophet ever yet has filled the place
Of Moses, who beheld God face to face.

Through him (the faithful in His house) the Lord
The law of truth to Israel did accord.

This law God will not alter, will not change
For any other through time's utmost range.

He knows and heeds the secret thoughts of man:
He saw the end of all ere aught began.

With love and grace doth He the righteous bless,
He metes out evil unto wickedness.

He at the last will His anointed send,
Those to redeem, who hope, and wait the end.

God will the dead to life again restore.
Praised be His glorious Name for evermore!

OLD HUNDRED

This hymn is so widely known and used that the word "Old" in the title can readily be a term of endearment or familiarity. At the same time, however, the music is old—at least 600 years old. It first appeared in psalters as the accompaniment to the Hundredth Psalm. The words still are in the spirit of that psalm, to which the Christian doxology has been added.

BE THOU, O God, exalted high,
   And as Thy glory fills the sky,
So let it be on earth displayed
   'Til Thou art here, as there, obeyed.

With one consent let all the earth
   To God their cheerful voices raise;
Glad homage pay with awful mirth,
   And sing before Him with songs of praise.

For He's the Lord, supremely good;
   His mercy is forever sure;

His truth, which always firmly stood,
  To endless ages shall endure.

Praise God, from Whom all blessings flow,
Praise Him, all creatures here below;
Praise Him above, ye heavenly host:
Praise Father, Son, and Holy Ghost.

MORNINGE PRAYER

This prayer is selected from the Book of Common Order, *printed in Geneva in 1556 for the English-speaking congregation which gathered there under the ministry of John Calvin. It is ascribed to several of the early Reformers, including* JOHN KNOX, *who introduced it into Scotland where it became known as "Knox's liturgy." I have followed the original spelling, including capitalization, as far as possible, making only minor changes where the sense might be lost. One example is the spelling out of "and." In the original, the word is spelled "âd"—the circumflex mark indicating the omission of the letter "n."*

ALMIGHTIE GOD, and most merciful father, we do not present our selves here before thy Majesty trusting in our mercies or worthyness, but in thy manifold mercies, which hast promised to heare our prayers and graunt our requestes, which we shall make to thee in the name of thy beloved sonne Jesus Christ our lord: who hath also commaunded us to assemble our selves together in his name, with ful assurance that he wyll not only be amongst us, but also be our mediator, and advocate towards thy Majestie, that we may obteyne all things which shall seme expedient to thy blessed wyll, for our necessities. Therefor we

beseche thee most mercifull father, to tourne thy lovynge con-
tenance towards us, and impute not unto us our many fold
synnes, and offences, whereby we justely deserve thy wrath and
sharpe punishement, but rather receyve us to thy mercy for
Jesus Christes sake, acceptinge his death and passion as a juste
recompense, for all our offences, in whome onely, thou art pleased
and through whome thou canst not be offended with us. And
seeinge that of thy great mercies, we have quietly passed this
night, graunt (O heavenly father) that we may spend and
bestowe this day wholy in thy service, so that all our thoughtes,
wordes, and deedes, may redounde to the glorie of thy name,
and good ensample to all men: who seeinge our good workes,
may glorifie thee our heavenly father.

PSALM 84

How amiable are Thy tabernacles, O Lord of hosts!
My soul longeth, yea, even fainteth for the courts of the Lord:
my heart and my flesh crieth out for the living God.

Yea, the sparrow hath found a house, and the swallow a nest
for herself, where she may lay her young, even Thine altars, O
Lord of hosts, my King, and my God.

Blessed are they that dwell in Thy house: they will be still
praising Thee. Selah.

Blessed is the man whose strength is in Thee; in whose heart
are the ways of them.

Who passing through the valley of Baca make it a well; the
rain also filleth the pools.

They go from strength to strength, every one of them in Zion
appeareth before God.

O Lord God of hosts, hear my prayer: give ear, O God of
Jacob. Selah.

Behold, O God our shield, and look upon the face of Thine anointed.

For a day in Thy courts is better than a thousand. I had rather be a doorkeeper in the house of my God, than to dwell in the tents of wickedness.

For the Lord God is a sun and shield: the Lord will give grace and glory: no good thing will He withhold from them that walk uprightly.

O Lord of hosts, blessed is the man that trusteth in Thee.

PRAYER FOR
A SICK PERSON

FATHER of mercies and God of all comfort, our only help in time of need; we humbly beseech Thee to behold, visit, and relieve Thy sick servant, ..., for whom our prayers are desired. Look upon him/her with the eyes of Thy mercy; comfort him/her with a sense of Thy goodness; preserve him/her from the temptations of the enemy; and give him/her patience under his/her affliction. In Thy good time, restore him/her to health, and enable him/her to lead the residue of his/her life in Thy fear, and to Thy glory; and grant that finally he/she may dwell with Thee in life everlasting; through Jesus Christ our Lord. Amen.

THANKSGIVING FOR
RECOVERY FROM SICKNESS

GOD, Who art the giver of life, of health, and of safety; we bless Thy Name, that Thou hast been pleased to deliver from his/her bodily sickness this Thy servant, who now desireth to return thanks unto Thee, in the presence of all Thy people. Gracious art Thou, O Lord, and full of compassion to the children of men. May his/her heart be duly impressed with a sense of Thy merciful goodness, and may he/she devote the residue of his/her days to a humble, holy, and obedient walking before Thee; through Jesus Christ our Lord. Amen.

PRAYER FOR SOCIAL JUSTICE

ALMIGHTY GOD, Who hast created man in Thine own image; grant us grace fearlessly to contend against evil, and to make no peace with oppression, and, that we may reverently use our freedom, help us to employ it in the maintenance of justice among men and nations, to the glory of Thy holy Name; through Jesus Christ our Lord. Amen.

LABOR DAY PRAYER

This prayer is from PASTOR H. M. TIPPETT *of the Seventh Day Adventist Church, who delivered it at a union meeting of printers—a "chapel," as the printers call it.*

GOD our Savior, author of faith and arbiter of human destiny, for the vigor of mind and strength of body and will to labor that brings us together today, we thank Thee. Thou hast filled the earth with Thy creative wisdom, and morning by morning Thy faithfulness is revealed in cooling breeze and sunlit horizon. Help us to be inwardly sensitive to all that is beautiful that we may be outwardly responsive to the impulses of Thy Spirit. Day by day we are awakened to recurring tokens of Thy care. In temporal needs Thou art our provider, in every lack our sufficiency, in every suffering our peace, in disappointment our hope. In our confrontation with evil or adversity, may we never forget that Thou art only a prayer away. Give us, then, this day the confidence that like Hagar in the wilderness we may look up into Thy face and say, "Thou, God, seest me." Let Thy love abound in our service and in our interpersonal relationships. Implement our skills for the work of each hour. And at the end of the day may we have that sense of fulfillment that comes from the knowledge that we have been working with Thee. We ask in Jesus' Name. Amen.

PRAYER FOR HELP
IN ONE'S VOCATION

ST. THOMAS AQUINAS, *the great 13th century philosopher, is so well known for his brilliant theological writings that his personal piety and devotion are frequently overlooked. This prayer is one of many he wrote.*

RANT ME, I beseech Thee, almighty and most merciful God, fervently to desire, wisely to search out, and perfectly to fulfill, all that is well pleasing unto Thee. Order Thou my worldly condition to the glory of Thy Name; and, of all that Thou requirest me to do, grant me the knowledge, the desire, and the ability, that I may so fulfill it as I ought, and may my path to Thee, I pray, be safe, straightforward, and perfect to the end.

Give me, O Lord, a steadfast heart, which no unworthy affection may drag downwards; give me an unconquered heart, which no tribulation can wear out; give me an upright heart, which no unworthy purpose may tempt aside.

Bestow upon me also, O Lord my God, understanding to know Thee, diligence to seek Thee, wisdom to find Thee, and a faithfulness that may finally embrace Thee. Amen.

PRAYER FOR FERVOR

JOHN HENRY CARDINAL NEWMAN, *author of this prayer, might best be described as a gentle zealot. An ardent crusader in the Church of England, he climaxed that career by converting to the Roman Catholic Church, and found himself in the unhappy role of an apostate. Eventually, however, his writings and his life had the happy result of easing the conflict between the peoples of both churches.*

TEACH ME, O Lord, and enable me to live the life of saints and angels. Take me out of the langor, the irritability, the sensitiveness, the anarchy, in which my soul lives, and fill it with Thy fullness. Breathe on me with that breath which infuses energy and kindles fervor. In asking for fervor, I ask for all that I can need, and all that Thou canst give. In asking for fervor, I am asking for faith, hope and charity, in their most heavenly exercise; I am asking for that loyal perception of duty which follows on yearning affection; I am asking for sanctity, peace, and joy, all at once. Nothing would be a trouble to me, nothing a difficulty, had I but fervor of soul. Lord, in asking for fervor, I am asking for Thyself, for nothing short of Thee, O my God. Enter my heart, and fill it with fervor by filling it with Thee. Amen.

JESUS, THE VERY THOUGHT OF THEE

The original of this hymn was by St. Bernard of Clairvaux, *celebrated monk of the 12th century. Gioachimo Rossini, whose career as a composer of operas ran from the 18th to the 19th centuries, wrote a musical accompaniment for it.*

Jesus, the very thought of Thee
With sweetness fills the breast;
But sweeter far Thy face to see,
And in Thy presence rest.

Nor voice can sing, nor heart can frame,
Nor can the memory find,
A sweeter sound than Jesus' Name,
The Savior of mankind.

O hope of ev'ry contrite heart,
O joy of all the meek,
To those who fall, how kind Thou art!
How good to those who seek!

STUDENT'S PRAYER

God, Who hast ordained that whatever is to be desired should be sought by labor, and Who, by Thy blessing, bringest honest labor to good effect; look with mercy upon my studies and endeavors. Grant me, O Lord, to design only what is lawful and right; and afford me calmness of mind, and steadiness of purpose, that I may so do Thy will in this short life as to obtain happiness in the world to come, for the sake of Jesus Christ our Lord. Amen.

PRAYER FOR KNOWLEDGE

This prayer comes from St. John Chrysostom, *archbishop of Constantinople in the fourth century and a Greek Father of the Church. The name "Chrysostom"—golden-mouthed—is a sobriquet given to him after his death in tribute to his eloquence.*

Almighty God, Who hast given us grace at this time with one accord to make our common supplications unto Thee; and dost promise that when two or three are gathered together in Thy Name Thou wilt grant their requests; fulfil now, O Lord, the desires and petitions of Thy servants, as may be most expedient for them; granting us in this world knowledge of Thy truth, and in the world to come life everlasting. Amen.

A PRAYER FOR PARENTS

This prayer was submitted by the REVEREND DOCTOR STANLEY
RABINOWITZ, *Rabbi of Adas Israel Synagogue, in Washington,*
D.C.

UR GOD and God of our Fathers, we thank Thee for
our children who have grown to manhood and womanhood.
In the trials and successes that come to them out in the world
of struggle, guard them, we pray, from self-seeking and keep
them true to the pledge of their youth, to serve humanity and
Thee.

Unveil to them Thy inspiration so that they may ever serve
Thee with integrity and the teaching of Thy prophets with
faithfulness. May we be given the understanding to grant to our
children that which they require for growth and maturity and
the courage to withhold from them that which we know will
do them harm. May we have the wisdom to guide them now,
and the fortitude to free them, when the time comes, to go
firmly and proudly on the way that they shall choose. Amen.

PRAISE TO GOD

LESSED, praised and glorified, exalted, extolled and
honored, magnified and lauded be the Name of the Holy One,
blessed be He; though He be high above all the blessings and
hymns, praises and consolations, which are uttered in the world;
and say ye, Amen.

[130]

PRAYER FOR GOOD
CHEER AND HAPPINESS

This is a prayer by the Reverend William Ellery Channing, *the famed pastor of Boston's Federal Street Church in the early 19th century: an early abolitionist and a pioneer in the temperance movement.*

God, animate us to cheerfulness. May we have a joyful sense of our blessings, learn to look on the bright circumstances of our lot, and maintain a perpetual contentedness under Thy allotments. Fortify our minds against disappointment and calamity. Preserve us from despondency, from yielding to dejection. Teach us that no evil is intolerable but a guilty conscience; and that nothing can hurt us, if, with true loyalty of affection, we keep Thy commandments, and take refuge in Thee. Amen.

PRAYER FOR STRENGTH
AND SELF-DENIAL

Lord, give us more charity, more self-denial, more likeness to Thee. Teach us to sacrifice our comforts to others, and our likings for the sake of doing good. Make us kindly in thought, gentle in word, generous in deed. Teach us that it is better to give than to receive; better to forget ourselves than to put ourselves forward; better to minister than to be ministered unto. And unto Thee, the God of Love, be glory and praise for ever. Amen.

BENEDICTUS ES, DOMINE

Blessed art Thou, O Lord God of our fathers: praised and exalted above all for ever.

Blessed art Thou for the Name of Thy majesty: praised and exalted above all for ever.

Blessed art Thou in the temple of Thy holiness: praised and exalted above all for ever.

Blessed art Thou that beholdest the depths, and dwellest between the cherubim: praised and exalted above all for ever.

Blessed art Thou on the glorious throne of Thy kingdom: praised and exalted above all for ever.

Blessed art Thou in the firmament of heaven: praised and exalted above all for ever. Amen.

PRAYER FOR A BLESSED DEATH

This prayer is attributed to PHILIPP MELANCHTHON, *a close friend and ally of Dr. Martin Luther. He is generally considered the prime theologian of the Lutheran reform movement and, as the author of the "Augsburg Confession," might well be considered the prototype of the many churchmen who have since pursued the goal of Ecumenism.*

Almighty and holy Spirit, the Comforter, pure, living, true—illuminate, govern, sanctify me, and confirm my heart and mind in the faith, and in all genuine consolation; preserve and rule over me that, dwelling in the house of the Lord all the days of my life, I may come to behold the beauty of the temple of the Lord, and praise Him with a joyful spirit, in union with all the heavenly church. Amen.

MORNING PRAYER

This prayer was written by a radio preacher of the Seventh Day Adventist Church: Pastor H. M. S. Richards, *of the Voice of Prophecy, in Glendale, California.*

UR Father in heaven, hear this our morning prayer. "It is of Thy mercies that we are not consumed, because Thy compassions fail not. They are new every morning: great is Thy faithfulness" (*Lamentations iii, 22–23*).

We thank Thee for Thy goodness to us revealed every day and in a thousand ways. We thank Thee for life, for health, friends, work and play. And above all else we thank Thee for love, human love and Thy love revealed in redeeming grace through Jesus Christ our Lord.

We thank Thee for Thy wonderful revelation in nature itself, in Thy providence and in the heart of man and in the Holy Scriptures. For Thy redeeming grace revealed in Jesus Christ our Lord we praise Thee and worship Thee. Forgive our sins we pray. Deliver us from the evil of our own hearts. Make us more like Him Whose Name above every name was Jesus.

We pray that Thou wilt extend Thy healing mercies to the sick, comfort them and remember those in any kind of trouble and lead us to help them to the extent of our ability. We pray for the peace of the world, and the peace of our homes and the peace of our hearts and for the preaching of Thy wonderful Word in all the world and to all men and to all nations. We pray for the rulers of the world. For it is written in Thy word that the king's heart is in the Lord's hand.

Help us to learn to live together in this Thy world so that we may indeed live together with Thee in Thy coming wonder world of the future. We pray that we may each become a blessing to others. And so we say from our hearts, glory be to Thee our Father in heaven and to Thy Son our Lord Jesus Christ and to the Holy Ghost for ever and ever. Amen.

A NIGHT PRAYER

BLESSED BE the Lord by day; blessed be the Lord by night; blessed be the Lord when we lie down; blessed be the Lord when we rise up. For in Thy hand are the souls of the living and the dead, as it is said, In His hand is the soul of every living thing, and the spirit of all human flesh. Into Thy hand I commend my spirit; Thou hast redeemed me, O Lord God of truth. Our God Who art in heaven, assert the unity of Thy Name, and establish Thy kingdom continually, and reign over us for ever and ever.

May our eyes behold, our hearts rejoice, and our souls be glad in Thy true salvation, when it shall be said unto Zion, Thy God reigneth. The Lord reigneth; the Lord hath reigned; the Lord shall reign for ever and ever: for the kingdom is Thine, and to everlasting Thou wilt reign in glory; for we have no king but Thee. Blessed art Thou, O Lord, the King, Who constantly in His glory will reign over us and over all His works for ever and ever. Amen.

PRAYER FOR
EVERY MAN IN HIS WORK

LMIGHTY GOD, our heavenly Father, Who declarest Thy glory and showest forth Thy handiwork in the heavens and in the earth; deliver us, we beseech Thee, in our several callings, from the service of mammon, that we may do the work which Thou givest us to do, in truth, in beauty, and in righteousness, with singleness of heart as Thy servants, and to the benefit of our fellow men; for the sake of Him Who came among us as One that serveth, Thy Son Jesus Christ our Lord. Amen.

PRAYER FOR ELECTION DAY

This selection is from the prayers of the REVEREND DOCTOR EDLER G. HAWKINS, *minister at St. Augustine Presbyterian Church, in New York City's Borough of the Bronx, Co-Chairman of the Council on Church and Race of the United Presbyterian Church in the United States of America.*

LMIGHTY GOD, Who has set before us the distinctions between good and evil, help us now through these days as we come to the place of choosing those who will lead and guide us. Confirm our devotion to the idea that a public office is truly a public trust. Make those who are elected sensitive instruments to do Your will, people with power, but people also with wisdom, lest they be an unwitting part in man's further inhumanity to

[135]

man. Put from them, and us, temptations of greed that set men one from another in silly quests after ends that will but confound us further and delay Your purpose for all men. Give them, and us, no pride in outworn ways, or a blindness that sees no need for change. Help them, and us, to see beneath our differences, our common needs. Open our understandings to Your knowledge that beneath our hunger for one another is yet a deeper hunger which only Your spirit can fill.

Guide us in some of the unknown corridors down which we ought to go, and make us ready for the thoughts that will rule the future, even if you must do it through our obstinate desire not to be disturbed.

Give us all a faith that Your power is never fully absent, but forever prompting men and women and young people to do the finest things in the most dismal times. And as we pray for the occasion of a new revelation our hope is that, under God, the cities of our time may become something like cities in which a good God dwells.

In the Name and in the spirit of Jesus Christ we humbly pray.

GOD OF OUR FATHERS

This prayer was selected from the prayers of PASTOR GEORGE E. VANDEMAN, *Director and Speaker of "It is Written," an apostolate of the Seventh Day Adventist Church in the broadcasting field in Washington, D.C.*

GOD of our fathers, Author of Liberty, to Thee we pray. To Thee we sing. To Thee we commit our souls because they are free, because we live in a land that is free, a universe that the Son of God died to keep free. Accept this consecration now in our Savior's Name. Amen.

A PRAYER OF THANKSGIVING

The REVEREND DOCTOR J. H. JACKSON, *President of the National
Baptist Convention, U. S. A., submitted this prayer.*

SPIRIT of the universe, Creator of the ends of the earth, and God of all life and destiny; we thank Thee for every blessing that has descended upon us.

We confess our unworthiness and our imperfections, but we rejoice in the limitless outreach of Thy grace, and the plentitude of Thy divine mercies. Keep us from pride and self-centeredness, and lead us always in Thy path of rectitude and righteousness, through Jesus Christ our Lord. Amen.

THANKSGIVING DAY PRAYER

LORD of the universe and Protector of all mankind, from Thee come all our blessings from day to day and from year to year. How great is Thy loving-kindness, O God. The sheltering mountains and the shaded forests, the abundant streams and the fruitful earth tell of Thy bountiful goodness.

In this land of ours so richly blessed by Thee, we raise our voice in joyous thanks. To these shores Thy children have come from many climes seeking liberty and a new hope in life. All have been pilgrims to this western world. Here they found renewed purpose, increased strength and the opportunity to outgrow old fears and suspicions. For America, for the freedom of its laws, the richness of its natural blessings and the growing

[137]

comradeship of its citizens, we praise Thee, O God, in humble thanksgiving. O, continue Thy loving-kindness to our beloved country. As Thou hast blessed it in the past, so renew Thy bounty in the years to come.

Praised be Thou, O Lord our God, King of the universe, Who causest the earth to yield food for all. Amen.

HARVEST PRAYER

OST GRACIOUS GOD, by Whose knowledge the depths are broken up, and the clouds drop down the dew; we yield Thee unfeigned thanks and praise for the return of seed-time and harvest, for the increase of the ground and the gathering in of the fruits thereof, and for all the other blessings of Thy merciful providence bestowed upon this nation and people. And, we beseech Thee, give us a just sense of these great mercies, such as may appear in our lives by an humble, holy, and obedient walking before Thee all our days; through Jesus Christ our Lord, to Whom, with Thee and the Holy Ghost, be all glory and honor, world without end. Amen.

A PRAYER
AGAINST GLUTTONY
AND DRUNKENESS

ARDON, O GOD, in whatsoever I have offended Thee by meat and drink and pleasures; and never let my body any more be oppressed with loads of sloth and delicacies, or my soul drowned in seas of wine or of strong drink; but let my appetites be changed into spiritual desires, that I may hunger after the food of angels and thirst for the wine of elect souls, and may account it meat and drink and pleasure to do Thy will, O God. Lord let me eat and drink so that my food may not become a temptation or a sin, or a disease; but grant that with so much caution and prudence I may watch over my appetite, that I may in the strength of Thy mercies, and refreshments, in the light of Thy countenance, and in the paths of Thy commandments, walk before Thee all the days of my life acceptable to Thee in Jesus Christ, ever advancing His honor, and being filled with His spirit, that I may at last partake of His glory, through the same Jesus Christ, our Lord. Amen.

GRACE BEFORE MEALS

Equal to man's almost instinctual prayer for his daily bread is the desire to thank God when you sit down to eat: to say a "grace." One of the most gracious Graces is this one, used frequently in the home of the RIGHT REVEREND JOHN E. HINES, *Presiding Bishop of the Episcopal Church.*

GOD, be Thou our unseen guest.
Fill our hearts with Thy love.
Make Thyself known to us
In the breaking of this bread.
In gratitude we ask it. Amen.

FATHER, GIVER OF ALL GOOD

This prayer was submitted by Pastor W. A. Fagal, *of the Seventh Day Adventist Church, speaker on the nationally telecast program "Faith for Today."*

UR Father, giver of all good, sharer of our sorrows and joys, grant us the wisdom to pray with hearts subdued with Thy love. Even though this world reels with wars, wickedness and the wreckage of sin, yet we know that Thy plans fail not. Help us today to be part of the solution to the problems of life and not part of the problems themselves.

May Thy love today extend to every human heart. To the soldier, wounded and dying on the battlefield; to the little child, crying forlornly in the ghetto; to the governor and the chief executive in the citadel of power; to the president of the great corporation, to the housewife and to the breadwinner. Bring to each the measure of strength essential to living the life of victory for Thee.

On this bruising pathway of life, we need a guide who knows the way—Thou art the guide. When life seems overfilled with trials and disappointments, we need comfort—Thou art the comforter. When we are caught in the steel traps of sin and habit, we need deliverance—Thou art the deliverer. Help us to equate life fully with the unchanging principles found in Thy word. May we remember that without daily communion with Thee our life is empty, our work meaningless, and our future unrewarding.

For everything that Thou art, we praise Thee and thank Thee. But, Father, in order to praise Thee rightly, we know we must yield the clay of our lives to be molded by Thy skilled hands into the symmetry of Thy attributes—love, peace, understanding, faith.

For Him Who came to bring us together, we thank Thee with the love and gratitude that only our Savior could give us. We love Jesus, Thy Son, because He first loved us, and left His place by Thy side to be by our side, to understand us, to live with us, to die for us. Help us to keep bright the blessed hope of His soon return, when the separations caused by sin will be forever removed.

As we ask these things in Christ's Name, we want to be filled with His love until there is enough not only for ourselves but for the whole world. In His Name we pray, Amen.

PSALM 150

RAISE ye the Lord. Praise God in His Sanctuary: praise Him in the firmament of His power.

Praise Him for His mighty acts: praise Him according to His excellent greatness.

Praise Him with the sound of the trumpet: praise Him with the psaltery and harp.

Praise Him with the timbrel and dance: praise Him with stringed instruments and organs.

Praise Him upon the loud cymbals: praise Him upon the high sounding cymbals.

Let every thing that hath breath praise the Lord. Praise ye the Lord.

THE PRAYER OF ANGELS

THE BLESSED GOD, great in knowledge, designed and formed the rays of the sun: it was a boon He produced as a glory to His Name: He set the luminaries around about His strength. The chiefs of His hosts are holy beings that exalt the Almighty, and continually declare the glory of God and His holiness. Be Thou blessed, O Lord our God, for the excellency of Thy handiwork, and for the bright luminaries which Thou hast made: they shall glorify Thee for ever: in tranquil joy of spirit, with pure speech and holy melody they all respond in unison, and exclaim with awe:

Holy, holy, holy is the Lord of hosts: the whole earth is full of His glory. Amen.

MORNING PRAYER

LORD, Who in infinite wisdom and love, orderest all things for Thy children, order everything this day for me in Thy tender pity. Thou knowest my weakness, Who madest me; Thou knowest how my soul shrinks from all pain of soul. Lord, I know Thou wilt lay no greater burden on me than Thou canst help me to bear. Teach me to receive all things this day from Thee. Enable me to commend myself in all things to please Thee; bring me through all things nearer unto Thee; bring me, day by day, nearer to Thyself, to life everlasting. Amen.

CHRISTMAS PRAYER

God, Who makest us glad with the yearly remembrance of the birth of Thine only Son Jesus Christ; grant that as we joyfully receive Him for our Redeemer, so we may with sure confidence behold Him when He shall come to be our Judge, Who liveth and reigneth with Thee and the Holy Ghost, one God, world without end. Amen.

A BENEDICTION

This prayer was submitted to Treasured Volume *by the* RIGHT REVEREND HORACE W. B. DONEGAN, *Bishop of New York.*

Go forth in peace.
Be of good courage.
Hold fast to that which is true.
Honor all men.
Be kind to one another.
Render no man evil for evil.
Do that which is good.
Comfort the afflicted.
Strengthen the weak-hearted.
Love and serve the Lord
   in the power and joy of the Holy Spirit.

And may the blessing of God Almighty, the Father, the Son, and the Holy Spirit be and abide with you and with all whom you love both on earth and in paradise now and ever more.

PRAYER FOR PEACE

O GOD, Who art the author of peace and lover of con-
cord, in knowledge of Whom standeth our eternal life, Whose
service is perfect freedom; defend us Thy humble servants in all
assaults of our enemies; that we, surely trusting in Thy defence,
may not fear the power of any adversaries, through the might of
Jesus Christ our Lord. Amen.

HYMN FOR
NEW YEAR'S DAY

WISDOM ascribe, and might, and praise,
   To God Who lengthens out our days,
Who spares us yet another year,
   And lets us see His goodness here.
Happy and wise, the time redeem,
   And live, my friends, and die to Him.

I, and my house, will serve the Lord,
   Led by the Spirit and the word;
We plight our faith, assembled here,
   To serve our God the ensuing year,
And vow, when time shall be no more,
   Through all eternity to adore.

[144]

PRAYER FOR THE YEAR'S END

ᴍost ɢʀᴀᴄɪᴏᴜs Goᴅ, Who hast been infinitely merciful to us, not only in the year past, but through all the years of our life, be pleased to accept our most unfeigned thanks for Thine innumerable blessings to us; graciously pardoning the manifold sins and infirmities of our life past, and bountifully bestowing upon us all those graces and virtues, which may render us acceptable to Thee. And every year which Thou shalt be pleased to add to our lives, add also, we humbly implore Thee, more strength to our faith, more ardor to our love, and a greater perfection to our obedience; and grant that in a humble sincerity and constant perseverance, we may serve Thee most faithfully the remainder of our lives, for Jesus Christ's sake. Amen.

PRAYER AT THE CLOSE OF A YEAR

ᴛᴇʀɴᴀʟ Jᴇʜᴏᴠᴀʜ, Whose nature is unchangeable, and of Whose years there is no end; we bless Thee that, amidst all the vicissitudes and dangers to which we are subject, Thou makest our lives Thy care. Hitherto the Lord hath helped us. We desire this day to call to remembrance the years of the Right Hand of the Most High. Goodness and mercy have followed us all the days of our lives. We would now particularly call to mind the mercies of the last year. We are the living, the living to praise Thee, as we do this day. Blessed be God for all the mercies, personal and relative, temporal and spiritual, with which the past year has been crowned. To Thy care, direction, and blessing we commit ourselves and each other for the following part of our lives, and especially for the year to come. We know not what even a day, much less a year, may bring forth: nor would we wish to know. It is enough for us to be assured that our times are in Thy hands. There we cheerfully leave ourselves and all our concerns, praying and believing that Thou wilt order all things wisely and graciously for us.

We pray, with submission to Thy sovereign will that Thou wouldst continue our lives, and preserve our health and comforts to the close of another year. But especially we pray that Thou wouldst prepare us for, and sanctify to us, the events of it, whatsoever they may be.

We would humbly lament the sins of the year past, as well as all the former sins of our lives. We beseech Thee of Thine infinite mercy, to pardon them; and grant us grace to watch and strive against the repetition of them. May all old things pass away, and all things become new.

We desire to begin the new year with You, God. We would freshly commit ourselves to Thy care, and consecrate ourselves to Thy service. And having done so, we desire cheerfully to refer all future events to Thine infinite wisdom, and fatherly goodness.

As each year which passes brings us nearer to death and eternity, may it find us better prepared for our great change. We know not but this year may be our last. God grant that it may prove our best. If Thou hast so decreed that this year any of us shall die, O grant that death may be no terror nor surprise to us. May we be dying daily to sin and the present world, so that whenever we finish this mortal life, we may enter upon that infinitely happy one which shall never end. May the close of every year, and every day, find us wiser and better: more happy in ourselves, more useful to others, and more fit for that world where days and years shall be unknown, and time shall be no more. In Thy presence may we there all spend a blessed eternity.

[146]

THE LORD IS MY SHEPHERD

The Psalms are generally regarded as among the greatest prayers ever written. But of all the 150, the greatest favorite seems to be this, the Twenty-third.

HE LORD is my shepherd—
  I shall not want:
He maketh me to lie down in green pastures;
  He leadeth me beside still waters.
He restoreth my soul;
  He guideth me in the paths of righteousness for His name's
    sake.
Yea, though I walk through the valley of the shadow of death
  I will fear no evil; for Thou art with me;
  Thy rod and Thy staff, they comfort me.
Thou preparest a table before me in the presence of mine ene-
    mies:
  Thou has anointed my head with oil;
  My cup runneth over.
Only goodness and loving kindness shall follow me all the days
    of my life.
  And I shall dwell in the house of My Lord for ever.

INDEX OF PRAYERS BY SUBJECT

AND

INDEX OF CONTRIBUTORS

INDEX OF
PRAYERS BY SUBJECT

INDEX OF CONTRIBUTORS

John Scott, a native of Trenton, New Jersey, has for a quarter of a century been with Radio Station WOR, where he is currently a newscaster and the focal man of the magazine-type program "Radio New York." A graduate in journalism from Kent State University, Scott—after his Army service—joined WOR and announced, directed, or produced a number of local and network radio and television shows in the news and documentary field while covering news stories that ranged from riots to medical conventions and even took him overseas. Scott maintains an active role in religious and civic activities. He is married, the father of two children, and lives—as he works—in the heart of Manhattan.

This book was designed for Oak Tree Press by Ernst Reichl. The type used is Granjon. The book was set by Atlantic Linotype Company in Brooklyn and produced by The Book Press Incorporated in Brattleboro, Vermont.